Success Books For Teens

THE NEXT 10 YEARS

What Every Teenager Should
Know Going Into The Next
Phase Of Life

Tomas Sharp

Table of Contents

Chapter 1:

7 Reasons Your Beliefs Are Holding You Back

You know that you have immense potential in your heart, and you are also working hard to attain your desired results, but something still doesn't fit right. Your beliefs might be consciously or unconsciously sabotaging your potential through your actions. This might create the less-than-desirable results that are holding you back from your real success.

Here are some 5 beliefs that might be getting in your way. Observe and analyze them, and start getting rid of them so that your path to success becomes easy and thorn-free.

C

1. Beliefs Are More Powerful Than You Think

"Beliefs have the power to create and the power to destroy. Human beings have the awesome ability to take any experience of their lives and create a meaning that disempowers them or one that can literally save their lives." - Tony Robbins. To change our lives, we first have to change our mindset and what we believe in so dearly. Challenging your beliefs is the key element to improve yourself. If we look around us, we might find a few limiting beliefs in the blink of an eye.

2. Everyone will get ahead of me if I rest.

This is perhaps the most crucial limiting belief that the majority of people go through. Many of us think that if we take some time off for ourselves, we'll fall behind in life, and everyone will get ahead of us, crushing us beneath them. For this particular reason, we stop focusing on our needs and necessities and burns out all of our energy on things that should come as second on our lists. Instead, we should convert our "shoulds" into "musts" and focus on ourselves too. Meditating for an hour, going to the gym, taking some time off for hanging out with friends or watching a movie alone, reading a book that's not connected to your work, these all are necessary to sustain life. Making excuses for not taking any time off for yourself and working day and night tirelessly will drain your energy or become a problem for your health; likewise, you will be tired physically and mentally and wouldn't be able to do your tasks on time.

3. Everyone is succeeding in life but me.

With the increasing social media norms and the lives of celebrities on every cover page, or seeing everyone around you figuring their lives out and enjoying themselves, you might feel that you are the only one who hasn't got a thing right. Unfortunately, human nature shows the world our successes and happiness rather than telling them our weak, struggling phases and vulnerability. Comparing yourself to those around you or any celebrity or influencer from social media may become a downward spiral for you when you are feeling confused and lost. Believing that everyone has it easy and you are the only one struggling could make you feel demotivated and depressed. This would, in turn, make you lazy, and you would eventually stop working towards your goal and passion.

4. I can never be good enough.

This limiting belief is the most common one among the people. Initially, they would give their all to a new job, a new relationship, or a new task. Then, if things wouldn't work out for them, they would just blame their performance and themselves and would label it as "I'm not good enough for this." This often leads to being anxious and finding perfection in things. And if failed to achieve this, one starts to procrastinate, thinking that their energies and efforts will eventually go to waste anyway. The little voice inside your head telling you that you're not good enough might also make you believe that you're not skilled enough or talented enough for the job or not deserving enough to be with the person you like. As a result, you pull yourself back and miss out on any opportunities offered to you.

5. I am capable enough to do everything myself.

We're often fooled by the idea that we don't need anyone's help, and we can figure out everything independently. This approach is majorly toxic as we all need a helping hand now and then. No one walks on the path of success alone. You may feel ashamed or guilty in asking for help or may think that you will be rejected or let down, or may think of yourself as the superior creature who knows everything and are not ready to listen to anyone else. All this might bring you down at one point in your life. We should always be open to any criticism and feedback and should never shy away from asking any help or advice from the people we trust and from the people we get inspired from.

6. The tiny voice becomes too loud sometimes

Limiting beliefs does impede us in some way. There's always this tiny voice in the back of our heads that keeps whispering thoughts and ideas into our minds. Most of what the voice tells us are negative stuff, and the worst part is that we actually start to believe in all of that. "You can never lose weight; stop trying. You're unattractive, and you won't find your significant other any time soon. You don't have the mindset or money to start up your own business; get yourself a 9-5 job instead." All of these, and much more, are what pulls us back from the things that we want to say or the stuff that we want to do.

7. The time isn't right.

The time isn't right, and believe me, it never will be. You're wasting your life away thinking that you will get married, lose your weight, learn a new skill, start your own business, all when the time will be correct. But there's no such as the right time. You either start doing what you want or sit on the side-lines and watch someone else do it. The right time is here and now. It would be best if you started doing the things you want until you make up your mind that you want to do it. You don't have to wait for a considerable amount of money to start a business; start with a small one instead. You don't have to settle down first to get married; find someone who will grow with you and help you. You don't need to spend hours and hours in the gym to lose weight; start eating healthy. There is no right time for anything, but the time becomes right when you decide to change yourself and your life for the better.

Conclusion:

You can make a thousand excuses or find a million experiences to back up your beliefs, but truth be told, you should always be aware of the assumptions you are creating and how they may be affecting your life. For example, will your beliefs stop you from taking action towards your life? Or will you change them into new and creative opportunities to get the results you want?

Chapter 2:

<u>Five Habits of A Healthy Lifestyle</u>

A healthy lifestyle is everybody's dream. The young and old, rich and poor, weak and strong, and male and female all want a happily ever after and many years full of life. The price to pay to achieve this dream is what distinguishes all these classes of people. What are you ready to forego as the opportunity cost to have a healthy lifestyle?

Here are five habits for a healthy lifestyle.

1. Eating Healthy Food

Your health is heavily dependent on your diet. You have heard that what goes inside a man does not defile him, but what goes out of him does. In this case, the opposite is true. What a man takes as food or beverage affects him directly. It can alter the body's metabolism and introduce toxins in the body hence endangering his life.

Most people do not take care of what they feed on. They eat anything edible that is readily available without any consideration. All other factors like the nutritive value of the food and its hygiene are secondary to most modern people who have thrown caution to the wind. Towns and cities are full of fast food joints and attract masses from all over. It is the most lucrative business these days. Are these fast foods healthy?

As much as the hygiene could be up to standards (due to the measures put in place by authorities), the composition of these foods (mostly chips and broiler chicken) is wanting. The cooking oil used is full of cholesterol that is a major cause of cardiac diseases. To lead a healthy lifestyle, eating healthy food should be a priority.

2. Regular Exercising

The human body requires regular exercise to be fit. Running, walking, swimming, or going to the gym are a few of the many ways that people can exercise. It is a call to get out of your comfort zone to ward off some lifestyle diseases. It is often misconstrued that exercising is a reserve for sportsmen and women. This fallacy has taken root in the minds of many people.

Unlearn the myths about exercises that have made most people shun them. The benefits of exercising are uncountable. It improves pressure and blood circulation in the body. Exercises also burn excess calories in tissues that would otherwise clog blood vessels and pose a health hazard. Research has shown that most people who exercise are healthy and fall sick less often. This is everyone's dream but the few who choose to pay the price enjoy it. Choose to be healthy by doing away with frequent motor vehicle transport and instead walk. A simple walk is an exercise already. When you fail to exercise early enough, you will be a frequent patient at the hospital. Prevention is always better than cure.

In the words of world marathon champion, Eliud Kipchoge, a running nation is a healthy nation.

3. Regular Medical Checkup

When was the last time you went for a medical checkup even when you were not sick? If the answer is negative or a long time ago, then a healthy lifestyle is still unreachable. A medical examination will reveal any disease in its early stages.

In most third-world countries, healthcare systems are not fully developed. Its citizens only go to the hospital when a disease has progressed and is in its late stages. At such a time, there is a higher probability of the patient succumbing to it. Doctors advise people to seek medical attention at the slightest symptom to treat and manage long-term illnesses. Regular medical checkups help one become more productive at work.

Is a healthy lifestyle attainable? Yes, it is when one takes the necessary measures to fight diseases. Regular medical checkups can be financially draining. Seek an insurance policy that can underwrite your health risks and this will make medical expenses affordable.

4. Staying Positive

A bad attitude is like a flat tire. If you do not change it, you will never go anywhere. There is a hidden power in having a positive attitude towards life. It all starts in the mind. When you conceive the right attitude towards life, you have won half the battle.

A healthy lifestyle starts with the mind. If you believe it, you can achieve it. So limitless is the human mind that it strongly influences the direction of a person's life. As much as there are challenges in life, do not allow them to conquer your mind or take over your spirit. Once they do, you will be constantly waging a losing battle. Is that what we want?

Associate with positive like-minded people and you will be miles away from depression and low self-esteem. We all desire that healthy lifestyle.

5. Have A Confidant And A Best Friend

Who is a best friend? He/she is someone you can trust to share your joy and sadness, and your high and low moments. You should be careful in your selection of a confidant because it may have strong ramifications if the friendship is not genuine.

A confidant is someone you can confide in comfortably without fear of him/her leaking your secrets. He/she will help you overcome some difficult situations in life. We all need a shoulder to lean on in our darkest times and a voice to comfort us that it is darkest before dawn. This helps fortify our mental health. We grow better and stronger in this healthy lifestyle.

These are the five habits for a healthy lifestyle. When we live by them, success becomes our portion.

Chapter 3:

Having a Balanced Life

Today we're going to talk about how and why you should strive to achieve a balanced life. A balance between work, play, family, friends, and just time alone to yourself.

We all tend to lead busy lives. At some points we shift our entire focus onto something at the expense of other areas that are equally important.

I remember the time when I just got a new office space. I was so excited to work that i spent almost 95% of the week at the office. I couldn't for the life of me figured why i was so addicted to going to the office that I failed to see I was neglecting my family, my friends, my relationships. Soon after the novelty effect wore off, i found myself burnt out, distant from my friends and family, and sadly also found myself in a strained relationship.

This distance was created by me and me alone. I had forgotten what my priorities were. I hadn't realized that I had thrown my life completely off balance. I found myself missing the time I spent with my family and friends. And I found myself having to repair a strained relationship due to my lack of care and concern for the other party.

What you think is right in the moment, to focus on something exclusively at the expense of all else, may seem enticing. It may seem like there is nothing wrong with it. But dig deeper and check to make sure it is truly worth the sacrifice you are willing to make in other areas of your life.

It is easy for us to fall into the trap of wanting to make more money, wanting to work harder, to be career driven and all that. But what is the point in having more money if you don't have anyone to spend in on or spend it with? What's the point in having a nice car or a nice designer handbag if you don't have anyone to show it to?

Creating balance in our lives is a choice. We have the choice to carve out time in our schedule for the things that truly matter. Only when we know how to prioritise our day, our week, our month, can we truly find consistency and stability in our lives.

I know some people might say disagree with what I am sharing with you all today, but this is coming from my personal life experience. It was only after realising that I had broken down all the things I had worked so hard to build prior to this new work venture, that I started to see the bigger picture again.

That I didn't want to go down this path and find myself 30 years later regretting that I had not spent time with my family before they passed away, that I was all alone in this world without someone I can lean my shoulder on to walk this journey with me, that I didn't have any friends that I could call up on a Tuesday afternoon to have lunch with me because everyone thought of me as a flaker who didn't prioritise them in the their lives before.

Choose the kind of life you want for yourself. If what I have to say resonates with you, start writing down the things that you know you have not been paying much attention to lately because of something else that you chose to do. Whether it be your lover, your friends, a hobby, a passion project, whatever it may be. Start doing it again. The time to create balance is now.

Chapter 4:

Happy People Create Time to Do What They Love Every Day

Most of our days are filled with things that we need to do and the things we do to destress ourselves. But, in between all this, we never get time for things. We wanted to do things that bring us pure joy. So then the question is, When will we find time to do what we love? Then, when things calm down a bit and when the people who visit us leave or finish all the trips we have planned and wrap up our busy projects, and the kids will be grown, we will retire? Then, probably after we are dead, we will have more time.

You do not have to wait for things to get less busy or calmer. There will always be something coming up; trips, chores, visitors, errands, holidays, projects, death and illness. There is never going to be more time. Whatever you have been stuck in the past few years, it will always be like that. So now the challenge is not waiting for things to change it is to make time for things you love no matter how busy your life is. Sit down and think about what you want to do, something that you have been putting off. What is something that makes you feel fulfilled and happy? Everyone has those few things that make them fall in love with life think of what is that for you. If you haven't figured it out yet, we will give you some examples, and maybe you can try some of these things and see how that makes you feel.

- Communing with nature

- Going for a beautiful walk

- Creating or growing a business or an organization

- Hiking, running, biking, rowing, climbing

- Meditating, journaling, doing yoga, reflecting

- Communing with loved ones

- Crafting, hogging, blogging, logging, vlogging
- Reading aloud to kids
- Reading aloud to kids

Did you remember something you enjoyed doing, but as the responsibilities kept increasing, you sidelined it. Well, this is your sign to start doing what you loved to take time out for that activity every day, even if it is for 30 minutes only. Carve that time out for yourself, do it now. Once you start doing this, you will realize that you will have more energy because your brain will release serotonin, and your energy level will increase. Secondly, your confidence will improve because you will be making something love every day, and that will constantly help you gain confidence because you will be putting yourself in a happy, self-loving state. You will notice that you have started enjoying life more when you do something you love once a day. It makes the rest of your day brighter and happier. You will also want to constantly continue learning and growing because your brain will strive to do more and more of the thing you like to do, and that will eventually lead to an increased desire of learning and growing. Lastly, your motivation will soar because you will have something to look forward to that brings you pure joy.

Chapter 5:

If Today Was Your Last Day

If today was your last day, what would you do with your life? Steve Jobs once said that "For the past 33 years, I have looked in trhe mirror every morning and asked myself: **'If today** were the **last day** of my life, would I want to do what I am about to do **today**? ' And whenever the answer has been 'No' for too many **days** in a row, I know I need to change something.".

Do you agree with that statement? For me I believe that it is true to a certain extent. I argue that not many of us have the luxury of doing what we love to do every single day. As much as we want to work at that dream job or earn that great salary, or whatever that ideal may be, for some of us who have to feed a family or make ends meet, it is just not possible. And we choose to make that sacrifice to work at a job that we may not like, or go through a routine that sometimes might seem a drag. But that's a personal choice that we choose to make and that is okay too.

On the flip side, i do believe that for those who have the luxury and the choice to pursue whatever careers, dreams, hobbies, and interests we want to pursue, that we should go for it and not live life in regret. I have heard of countless friends who work at a job they hate day in and day out, complaining about their life every single day and about how miserable they are, but are too afraid to leave that job in fear of not being able to find something they like or in fear that their dreams would not work out. Not because they couldn't afford to do so, but because they are afraid. This fear keeps them trapped in a never ending cycle of unhappiness and missed opportunities.

Personally, I'm in the camp of doing something you dislike even if u struggle with it if it can provide you with some financial security and pay your bills, whilst at the same time pursuing your dreams part time just to test the waters. You have the comfort of a monthly stream of income while also taking a leap of faith and going after what you really want to do in life. And who knows it could work out some day. In the present moment, I'm actually working on many different interests and hobbies. I do the necessary work that i hate but explore other areas that brings me joy, and that is what keeps be going. I have a passion for singing, songwriting, tennis, and making videos like this that not only educates but also aims to bring joy to others. My full-time job only fulfils my bank account while my interests and work that i do on the side fulfils my heart and soul. And who knows, if any one of these side hobbies turn out into something that I can make some money with, hey it's a win win situation now don't you think?

I challenge each and every one of you to go ahead and take a leap of faith. Time waits for no one and you never know when your last day might be. Koby Bryant died suddenly from a helicopter crash at a young age of 41. But I would argue that because he pursued his dreams at a young age, he has already lived a wonderful and fulfilling life as opposed to someone who is too afraid to do what they want and hasn't lived up to their fullest potential despite living until 90. You have also heard of Chadwick Boseman who was immortalised as a great human being who gave it his all despite fighting colon cancer. He pursued his dreams and I bet that he had no regrets that his life had to end earlier than it should. And to Steve jobs, he gave us Apple, the biggest company in the world by pursuing his dream of changing the world and the way we communicate with one another. Without him we wouldn't have all our favourite beloved apple products that we use today. Without him there might not be amazon, google, Facebook because there wouldn't be apps and there wouldn't be devices that people used to do all these things with.

But most importantly, this is about you. How do you want to live your life, and if today was your last day, what would you do differently and how would this carry on to all other areas of your life. Your relationships with your family, your relationship with your friends, your partner. And do you feel fulfilled as a human being or do you feel empty inside. It is never too late to turn your life around and make choices that will make your heart fill with immense joy and gratitude until your life truly ends. So make the decision right now to honour yourself by living your day to the fullest, coz you never know when it might be your last.

Chapter 6:

10 Habits That Make You More Attractive

Being attractive does not necessarily connote physical appearance. More than the physical appearance, attraction renders the mental, emotional, and spiritual energy irresistible to others. Some people radiate with their energy and confidence regardless of whether they have money, looks, or are socially connected. These people are just irresistible, and you will find that people will always approach them for advice, help, or even long-term companionships. What makes them more attractive? Their sense of self-worth is always from within their souls as contrasted with how they look from outside. They don't seek validation from others- but find it within themselves.

However, this is not genetically connected, but a habit that we can build within ourselves. You need to pursue and maintain such habits for the benefit of a greater you.

Here are 10 habits that make you more attractive:

1. **Connect With People More Deeply.**

Attractive people are always likable people, and being likable is a skill. Being likable means that you should be interested in hearing others out rather than spending all the time thinking and talking about yourself. As entrepreneur Jim Rohn puts it- "Irresistible or likeable people possess an authentic personality that enables them to concentrate more on those around them." This requires that you are in most cases over yourself, meaning that you don't spend more time only thinking about yourself.

To have this habit going on in you, try to take conversations seriously. Put that phone down and listen! Learn what those around you are into - Ask questions, enquire about their dreams, fears, preferences, and views on life. Focus on what is being said rather than what the response is or what impact that might have on you. Always aim to make others everyone feel valued and important.

2. **Treat Everyone With Respect.**

Being polite and unfailingly respectful is the key to being likable. If you are always rude to others, you will find that over time people will tend to avoid you. You should strive to not only be respectful to someone you know and like, but also to strangers that you come across with. Attractive people treat everyone with the same respect they deserve bearing in mind that no one is better.

3. **Follow the Platinum Rule.**

The commonly known version of the golden rule is that you should treat others the same way you want them to treat you. This comes with a major flaw: the assumption that everyone aspires to be treated similarly. The rule ignores the fact people are different and are motivated differently. For instance, one person's love for public attention is another's person's execrate. However, you can opt for this flaw by adopting the platinum rule instead. The notion is that you should only treat others as they want to be treated. Attractive people are good at reading others and quickly adjust to their style and behavior, and as a result, they can treat them in a way that makes them feel comfortable.

4. **Don't Try Too Hard To Put an Impression.**

Attractive people who are easily likable don't try too hard to impress. Liking someone comes naturally, and it depends on their personality. Hence if you spend most of the time bragging about your success or smartness, you are simply harming yourself without knowing it. People who try too hard to be liked are not likable at all. Instead they come across as narcissistic and arrogant. If you wish to be an attractive person choose to be humble and down-to-earth instead. People will see your worth with their own two eyes.

5. **Forgive and Learn From Your Mistakes.**

Learning from our mistakes is synonymous with self-improvement. It is proven that psychological traits are essential in human mating or relationships, meaning that both intelligence and kindness are key. Being intelligent, in this case, doesn't necessarily mean the PHDs or Degrees. It means that a person can demonstrate intelligence by learning from mistakes they make and handling the same well. You demonstrate this also by being kind to yourself whenever you make a mistake and avoiding the same mistake in the future. Attractive people know how to not take themselves too seriously and to have a laugh at themselves once in a while.

6. Smile Often

People tend to bond unconsciously with the body language portrayed while conversing. If you are geared towards making people more attracted to you, smile at them when conversing or talking to them. A smile makes other people feel comfortable in conversations, and in turn, they do the same to you. The feeling is remarkably good!

7. Likable People Are Authentic and Are Persons of Integrity.

People are highly attractive to realness. Attractive people portray who they are. Nobody has to expend energy or brainpower guessing their objective or predicting what they'll do next. They do this because they understand that no one likes a fake. People will gravitate toward you if you are genuine because it is easy to rely on you. On the flip side, it is also easy to resist getting close to someone if you don't know who they really are or how they actually feel.

People with high integrity are desirable because they walk their talk. Integrity is a straightforward idea, but it isn't easy to put into action. To show honesty every day, attractive people follow through with this trait. They refrain from gossiping about others and they do the right thing even if it hurts them to do so.

8. Recognize and Differentiate Facts and

Opinions.

Attractive people can deal gracefully and equally with divisive subjects and touchy issues. They don't shy away from expressing their views, but they clarify that they are just that: opinions, not facts. So, whenever you in a heated discussion, be it on politics or other areas with your peers, it is important to understand that people are different and are just as intelligent as you are. Everyone holds a different opinion; while facts always remain facts. Do not confuse the two to be the same.

9. Take Great Pleasure in The Little Things

Choose joy and gratitude in every moment – No matter if you are feeling sad, fearful, or happy. People who appreciates life for its up and downs will always appear attractive to others. Choose to see life as amazing and carefully approach it with joy and gratitude – Spread positive vibes and attract others to you that are also positive in nature. View obstacles as temporary, not inescapable. Everyone has problems, but it is how you deal with it each day that is important here. Optimistic people will always come out on top.

10. Treating friendships with priority.

True friendships are a treasure. When you take your time and energy to nourish true friendships, you will naturally develop others skills necessary to sustain all forms of relationships in your life. People will always gravitate to a person who is genuinely friendly and caring. They want to be a part of this person's life because it brings them support and joy. Take these friendships with you to the distance.

Bonus Tip: Do Your Best to Look Good.

There is a huge difference between presentation and vanity. An attractive person will always make efforts to look presentable to others. This is comparable to tidying up the house before you receive visitors - which is a sign of gratitude to others. Don't show up sloppily to meetups and parties; this will give others the impression that you don't care about how you look which may put off others from approaching you. Always try your best in every situation.

Conclusion: Bringing it all in

Attractive people don't get these habits simply floating over their beds. They have mastered those attractive characteristics and behaviors consciously or subconsciously - which anyone can easily adopt.

You have to think about other people more than you think about yourself, and you have to make others feel liked, appreciated, understood, and seen. Note, the more you concentrate on others, the more attractive you will appear and become without even trying.

Chapter 7:

Happy People Engage in Deep Meaningful Conversations

Psychologist Matthias Mehl and his team set out to study happiness and deep talk. In the journal Psychological Science, his study involved college students who wore an electronically activated recorder with a microphone on their shirt collar that captured 30-second snippets of conversation every 12.5 minutes for four days. Effectively, this created a conversational "diary" of their day.

Then researchers went through the conversations and categorized them as either small talk (talk about the weather, a recent TV show, etc.) or more substantive discussion (talk about philosophy, current affairs, etc.). Researchers were careful not to automatically label specific topics a certain way—if the speakers analyzed a TV show's characters and their motivations, this conversation was considered substantive.

The researchers found that about a third of the students' conversations were considered substantive, while a fifth consisted of small talk. Some conversations didn't fit neatly into either category, such as discussions that focused on practical matters like who would take out the trash.

The researchers also studied how happy the participants were, drawing data from life satisfaction reports the students completed and feedback from people in their lives.

The results? Mehl and his team found that the happiest person in the study had twice as many substantive conversations, and only one-third the small talk, as the unhappiest person. Almost every other conversation the happiest person had—about 46 percent of the day's conversations—was substantive.

As for the unhappiest person, only 22 percent of that individual's conversations were substantive, while small talk made up only 10 percent of the happiest person's conversations.

Does small talk equal unhappiness? Score one for Team Introvert because we've known this all along.

How to Have More Meaningful Conversations

instead of

- "How are you?"

- "How was your weekend?"

- "Where did you grow up?"

- "What do you do for a living?"

Try

- "What's your story?"

- "What was your favorite part of your weekend?"

- "Tell me something interesting about where you grew up."

- "What drew you to your line of work?"

Why Is Happiness Linked with Deep Talk?

Further research is still needed because it's not clear whether people make themselves happier by having substantive conversations or whether people who are already happy choose to engage in meaningful talk. However, one thing is evident: Happiness and meaningful interactions go hand-in-hand.

In an interview with the *New York Times*, Mehl discussed the reasons he thinks substantive conversations are linked to happiness. For one, humans are driven to create meaning in their lives, and substantive conversations help us do that, he said. Also, human beings—both introverts and extroverts—are social animals who have a real need to connect with others. Substantive conversation connects, while small talk doesn't.

Chapter 8:

Consistency Can Bring You Happiness

Happiness is an individual concept.

One man's riches is another man's rubbish.

As humans we are not happy if we do not have a routine, a reason to get up, and a purpose to live.

Without working towards something consistently, we become lost.

We begin to drift.

Drifting with no purpose eventually leads to emptiness.

When we are drifting in a job we hate,

We are trading our future away,

When we inconsistent in our relationships,

Problems are bound to arise.

Choose consistent focus instead.

Figure out exactly what you want and start to change it.

Employ consistent routines and habits that to move you towards your goals.

Consistency and persistence are key to success and happiness.

Without consistent disciplined effort towards what we want, we resign to a life of mediocrity.

Read a book for an hour consistently every single day.

You will become a national expert in 1 year.

In 5 years, a global expert.

That is the power of consistency.

Instead, people spend most of their free time scrolling through social media.

Consistency starts in the mind.

Control your thoughts to be positive despite the circumstances.

Nothing in the world can make us happy if we choose not to be.

Choose to be happy now and consistently working towards your goals.

We cannot be happy and successful if we dwell in the day to day setbacks.

We must consistently move like a bulldozer.

We have to keep going no matter what.

Nothing stays in the path of a bulldozer for too long.

In life, no matter where you are, you only ever have two choices.

Choose to stay where you are? Or choose to keep moving?

If where you are is making you happy, then by all means do more of it.

If not. What will? And why?

This should be clear before you take action.

Start with the end in your mind.

Let your body catch-up to it afterwards.

The end result is your what.

The action required is your how.

Concentrate on the what and the how and it will all be revealed soon enough.

Concentrate consistently on what you want for yourself and your family.

Distraction and lack of consistent action is a killer of happiness and success.

Your happiness is the life you want.

Take consistent action towards that life you've always dreamed of.

Commitment and endurance is part of that process.

On earth things need time to nurture and grow.

Everything in life depends on it.

The right conditions for maximum growth.

You can't just throw a seed on the concrete and expect it to grow with no soil and water,

Just as you can't simply wish for change and not create the right environment for success.

A seed requires not just consistent sunlight,

But the perfect combination of water and nutrients as well.

You might have given that seed sunlight,

just as you have your dream hope,

But without faith and consistent action towards the goal, nothing will happen.

The seed will still stay a seed forever.

Consistency in thought and action is everything towards happiness.
Nothing can grow without it.
Your success can be measured by your time spent working towards your goals.
If we consistently do nothing we become successful in nothing.
If we have to do something, should it not be something worth doing?

Start doing things that make you happy and fulfilled.
Consistency towards something that makes you happy is key towards lasting success.
Adapt when necessary but remain consistent with the end result in mind.
The path can be changed when necessary but the destination cannot.
Accepting anything less is admitting defeat.

Consistent concentration on the end result can and will be tested.
It however cannot be defeated, unless you quit.
If we remain steadfast in our belief that this is possible for us, it will be possible.
After a while things will seem probable. Eventually it becomes definite.

Continue to believe you can do it despite the circumstances.
Continue despite everyone around you saying you can't do it.

In spite of social status,
in spite of illness or disability,

in spite of age, race or nationality,

know you can do nearly anything if you consistently put all of your mind and body towards the task.

Take the pressure off.
There is no set guideline.
It is what you make of it.

There is no set destination or requirements.
Those are set my you.

The only competition is yourself from yesterday.
If you can consistently outperform that person, your success is guaranteed.
Consistent concentration and action towards your dream is key you your success and happiness.

Chapter 9:

<u>9 Habits of Highly Successful People</u>

Success comes to people who deserve it. I bet you have heard this statement quite a few times, right? So, what does it mean exactly? Does it mean that you are either born worthy or unworthy of success? Absolutely not. Everyone is born worthy, but the one thing that makes some people successful is their winning habits and their commitment to these habits.

Today, we will learn how to master ten simple habits and behaviors that will help you become successful.

1. Be an Avid Learner

If you didn't know, almost all of the most successful people in the world are avid learners. So, do not shy away from opportunities when it comes to learning. Wake up each day and look forward to learning new things, and in no time, I bet you will experience how enriching it really is. Also, learning new things has the effect of revitalizing a person. So, if you want to have more knowledge to kickstart your journey in the right direction, here are some things that you can do - make sure to read, even if it is just a page or two, daily. It could be anything that interests you. I personally love reading self-help books. If you are not that much of a reader, you can even listen to a podcast, watch an informative video, or sign up for a course. Choose what piques your interest, and just dive into it!

2. Failure is the Pillar of Success

Most people are afraid to delve into something new, start a new chapter of their lives, and chase after their dreams – all because they are scared to fail. If you are one of those people who are scared to fail, well, don't be! Because what failure actually does is prepares you to achieve your dream. It just makes sure that you are able to handle the success when you finally have it. So when you accept that failure is an inevitable part of your journey, you will be able to plan the right course of action to tackle it instead of just being too scared to move forward. Successful people are never scared of failure; They just turn it around by seeing it as an opportunity to learn.

3. Get Up Early

I bet you have heard this a couple of thousand times already! But whoever told you so was not lying. Almost all successful individuals are early risers! They say that starting the morning right ensures a fruitful day ahead. It is true! Think about it, on the day you get up early, you feel a boost of productivity as compared to when you wake up late and have to struggle against the clock. You will have plenty of time and a good mood to go through the rest of the day which will give you better outcomes. All you have to do is set up a bedtime reminder. This is going to make sure that you enough rest to get up in the morning instead of snoozing your alarm on repeat! Not a morning person? Don't worry. I have got you covered! Start slow and set the alarm 15 minutes before when you usually wake up. It doesn't sound like much, eh? But trust me, you will be motivated to wake up earlier when you see how much difference 15 minutes can make to your day.

4. Have Your Own Morning Ritual

Morning rituals are the most common habit among achievers. It will pump you up to go through the day with a bang! You just have to make a routine for yourself and make sure to follow it every day. You can take inspiration from the morning routines of people you look up to but remember it has to benefit you. So you might be wondering, *What do I include in the ritual?* I would suggest you make your bed first thing in the morning. This might not sound as great a deal, but hey, it is a tested and approved method to boost your productivity. It is even implemented in the military. Doing this will motivate you as you get a sense of achievement as you have completed a task as soon as you woke up. After that, it could be anything that will encourage you, such as a walk, a workout session, reading, journaling, or meditating.

5. Stop Procrastinating

From delaying one task to not keeping up with your deadlines, procrastination becomes a deadly habit. It becomes almost unstoppable! Did you know, most people fail to achieve their dreams even if they have the potential just because of procrastination? Well, they do. And you might not want to become one of them. They say, "Old habits die hard," true, but they do die if you want them to. Procrastination has to be the hardest thing we have to deal with, even though we hey created it in the first place. Trust me, I speak from experience!

So what do you do to stop this? Break your task into small bite-sized pieces. Sometimes, it is just the heaviness of the task that keeps us from doing it. Take breaks in between to keep yourself motivated.

Another thing that you can do is the "minute rule." Divide your tasks by how much time they take. The tasks that take less than 5 minutes, you do it right then. Then you can bigger tasks into small time frames and complete them. Make sure you do not get too lost in the breaks, though!

6. Set Goals

I cannot even begin to tell you how effective goal setting is. A goal gives you the right direction and motivation. It also gives you a sense of urgency to do a task that is going to just take your productivity level from 0 to 10 in no time!

So how do you set goals? Simple. Think about the goals you want to achieve and write them down. But make sure that you set realistic goals. If you find it difficult, don't worry. Start small and slow. Start by making a to-do list for the day. You will find out soo that the satisfaction in ticking those off your list is unbelievable. It will also drive you to tick more of them off!

7. Make Your Health a Priority

Health is Wealth. Yes, it is a fact! When you give your body the right things and make it a priority, it gives you back by keeping you and your mind healthy. I bet you've heard the saying "You are what you eat," and by "eat," it does not simply mean to chew and swallow! It also means that you need to feed your body, soul, and mind with things you want them to be like. Read, listen, learn, and eat healthy. You could set a goal to eat clean for the week. Or workout at least for 10 minutes. And see for yourself how it gives you the energy to smash those goals you've been holding off! Also, great news – you can have cheat days once a week!

8. Plan Your Day the Night Before

"When you fail to plan, you plan to fail." People who succeed in life are not by mere coincidence or luck. It is the result of detailed, focused planning. So, you need to start planning your way to success too. Before you sleep tonight, ask yourself, *What is the most important thing that I have to do tomorrow?* Plan what assignments, meetings, or classes you have to complete. Planning ahead will not only make you organized and ready, it also highly increases your chances to succeed. So, don't forget to plan your day tonight!

9. Master the Habit Loop

Behavioral expert, BJ Fogg, explains that habits are formed around three elements: Cue, Routine, and Reward. Cue is the initial desire that motivates your behavior. Routine is the action you take. And the reward is the pleasure you gain after completion. So why am I telling you all of this? Because this habit loop is how we are wired. It is what motivates us. We seek pleasure and avoid pain. And you can use this loop to your advantage! Let's say you want to finish an assignment. Think of the reason why you want to. Maybe you don't want to fall behind someone or want to impress someone. It could be anything! Now time for you to set your rewards. It could be eating a slice of cheesecake or watching an episode of your favorite series after you've finished. Rewards motivate you when you slack off. Play around until you find a combination that works best for you. You will also need a cue; it could be anything like a notification on your phone, an email, or simply your desire. You can set a cue yourself by creating a reminder.

Habits are what make a man. I hope you follow these habits and start your journey the right way to becoming successful in life.

Chapter 10:

<u>10 Habits of Bernard Arnault</u>

Bernard Arnault- French investor, businessman, and CEO of LVMH recently reclaimed the title "worlds' wealthiest" from fellow billionaire Jeff Bezos. His business acumen and awe-inspiring financial achievements deserve to be recognized. His perspective can serve as a model for entrepreneurs who want to follow in his footsteps.

Bernard Arnault has written about money, prosperity, leadership, and power over the years. Moreover, his path to becoming the CEO of one of the world's most recognized brands will provide you with valuable lessons to emulate from. That is, your life circumstances shouldn't stop you from expanding and thriving outside your expertise.

Following his impressive accomplishments, here are ten points you can take away from Arnault's journey to success.

1. Happiness Before Money

According to Bernard, happiness is leading. That is leading your team to the top whether you are in business, sports, music industry. Money, according to him, is a consequence, and success is a blend of your past and future.

Your priority is not what you'll make sooner! When you put much-required effort into your job, profits will flow.

2. Mistakes Your Lesson

Your biggest mistake is your learning opportunity. When your business isn't performing well, understand the situation first and be patient.
In the world of innovative brands, it can take years to get something to work. Give it time and put yourself in a long-term expectation.

3. Always Behave as a Startup

Think small. Act quickly. Smaller boats can turn faster than more giant tankers. Arnault emphasizes the significance of thinking small. LVMH, in Arnault's opinion, is not a massive corporation device with miles of unnecessary bureaucracy.
Believe in your vision while attracting the best talent for your success path. A handy, adaptable speed, one that can fail quickly as easy to sleeve up.

4. Continuously Reinvent Yourself

How do you maintain your relevance? Bernard's LVMH is built on innovation, quality, entrepreneurship, and, essentially, on long-term vision. LVMH excels at developing increasingly desirable new products and selling them globally.
To be successful today, with your capabilities, opt for a worldwide startup and see what's going on. This necessitates a more considerable investment, which gives you an advantage. However, let the Creators run your inventions.

5. Team-Creative Control

Arnault strategies find creative control under each product's team to do what they do best. Arnault's designers are the dreamer's realists and critics. Allow your team to take creative control. You risk putting a tourniquet around their minds if you restrict them in any way.

6. Create Value To Attract Customers

Marketing investigates what the customer desires. As a result, you are doing what they need: creating a product and testing it to see if it works. Keeping your products in close contact with consumers, according to Arnault, makes a desire to buy in them. LVMH creates products that generate customers. For him, it's never about sales; it's always about creating desire. Your goal should be to be desirable for long-term marketability.

7. Trust the Process

There will always be different voices in business, and while there will undoubtedly be good advice, if you believe an idea will succeed, you may need to persevere until the end. Like Arnault, disregard your critics by following through with your vision to excel.

8. Your Persistence Is Everything

It would be best if you were very persistent. It would be best to have ideas, but the idea is only 20% of the equation. The execution rate is 80%.

So if you are trying out a startup, having ideas marvellous, the driving force is persistence and execution.

When it comes to the most successful startups, such as Facebook, the idea was great from the beginning. Others, however, had the same idea. So why is Facebook such a phenomenal success today? It is critically through execution with persistence.

9. Do Not Think of Yourself

Bernard Arnault can be differentiated from other billionaires like Elon Musk or Bill Gates by focusing on the brands, making their longevity rather than making himself the face. He is only concerned with promoting his products.

To accomplish this, you must maintain contact with pioneers and designers, for example, while also making their ideas more specific and sustainable.

10. Maintain Contact With Your Company

One of the most common leadership mistakes is to lose sight of the company once you reach the top and "stick" with manageable goals. Instead, to see if the machine is working correctly or if there is room for improvement, you must examine every corner and every part of it.

Conclusion

Your willingness to outwork and your ability to outlearn everyone will keep your success journey intact and going. Bernard Arnault's path to becoming the CEO of the worlds most recognized and desired multi-billion empire of brands have a valuable lesson for you: your starting point does not influence or determine your future destination.

Chapter 11:

Planning Ahead

The topic that are going to discuss today is probably one that is probably not going to apply to everybody, especially for those who have already settled down with a house, wife, kids, a stable career, and so on. But i still believe that we can all still learn something from it. And that is to think about planning ahead. Or rather, thinking long term.

You see, for the majority of us, we are trained to see maybe 1 to 2 years ahead in our lives. Being trained to do so in school, we tend to look towards our next grade, one year at a time. And this system has ingrained in us that we find it hard to see what might and could happen 2 or 3 years down the road.

Whilst there is nothing wrong with living life one year at a time, we tend to fall into a short term view of what we can achieve. We tell ourselves we must learn a new instrument within 1 year and be great at it, or we must get this job in one year and become the head of department, or we must find our partner and get married within a short amount of time. However, life does not really work that way, and things actually do take much longer, and we do actually need more time to grow these small little shoots into big trees.

We fail to see that we might have to give ourselves a longer runway time of maybe 3-5 or even 10 years before we can become masters in a new instrument, job, relationship, or even friendships. Rome isn't built in a day and we shouldn't expect to see results if we only allow ourselves 1 year to accomplish those tasks. Giving ourselves only 1 year to achieve the things we want can put unnecessary pressure on ourselves to expect results fast, when in reality no matter how much you think u think rushing can help you achieve results faster, you might end up burning yourself out instead.

For those short term planners, even myself. I have felt that at many stages in my life, i struggle to see the big picture. I struggle to see how much i can achieve in lets say 5 years if i only allowed myself that amount of time to become a master in whatever challenge i decide to take on. Even the greatest athletes take a longer term view to their career. They believe that if they practice hard each day, they might not expect to see results in the first year, but as their efforts compound, by the 5th year they would have already done so much practice that it is statistically impossible not to be good at it.

And when many of us fall into the trap of simply planning short term, our body reacts by trying to rush the process as well. We expect everything to be fast fast fast, and results to be now now now. And we set unrealistic goals that we cannot achieve and we beat ourselves up for it come December 31st.

Instead i believe many of us should plan ahead by giving ourselves a minimum of 2.5 years in whatever task we set to achieve, be it an income goal, a fitness goal, or a relationship goal. 2.5 years is definitely much more manageable and it gives us enough room to breathe so that we don't stress ourselves out unnecessarily. If you feel like being kinder to yourself, you might even give yourselves up to 5 years.

And again the key to achieving success with proper long term planning is Consistency. If you haven't watched my video on consistency do check it out as i believe it is one of the most important videos that I have ever created.

I believe that with a run time of 5 years and consistency in putting the hours every single day, whether it is an hour or 10 hours, that by the end of it, there is no goal that you cannot achieve. And we should play an even longer game of 10 years or so. Because many of the changes we want to make in life should be permanent and sustainable. Not a one off thing.

So I challenge each and everyone of you today to not only plan ahead, but to think ahead of the longevity of the path that you have set for yourself. There is no point rushing through life and missing all the incredible sights along the way. I am sure you will be a much happier person for it.

Chapter 12:

Happy People Reward Themselves

Do you ever wonder if the carrot and stick principle would still work in this world? The answer to this would be yes, the reward and punishment system still works, and you can always leverage it to build good habits. They, in turn, will help you reach your goal faster; that is why it is essential to celebrate your hard work and then afterward reward yourself for the effort you have been putting in. Gretchen Rubin, in her book Better than before, says,

"When we give ourselves treats, we feel energized, cared for, and contented, which boosts our self-command — and self-command helps us maintain our healthy habits."

If you do not get any rewards and treats, you will feel resentful angry, and you feel depleted. Imagine putting in all the hard work and then not getting anything in return. How would that make you feel? Bad, right? That is precisely why rewarding yourself is essential. We are going to outline 2 simple reasons why rewarding yourself is important.

1. Reward makes you feel good and drives you further.

How do you train pets, your dogs, and cats? You teach them with a treat. Just like them, our brain works the same way we can train ourselves to do a lot more work by rewarding ourselves. When you give yourself a treat, you will boost your mood, making you happy. When you give yourself a treat, your brain releases a chemical called dopamine that makes you feel good and happy. Even tho it is important to reward yourself, not all rewards give the same effect, and you should choose wisely so that those treats create positive reinforcement.

2. It works as positive reinforcement.

When a pleasant outcome follows your behavior, you are more likely to repeat the behavior. And this is called positive reinforcement. Connecting your hard work to rewards effectively not only gives you a mental break but also motivates you to want to do more of it. Therefore, use treats as positive reinforcement to build your momentum and grow your habits.

Just like this powerful saying from Tony Robbins:

"People who succeed have momentum. The more they succeed, the more they want to succeed, and the more they find a way to succeed. Similarly, when someone is failing, the tendency is to get on a downward spiral that can even become a self-fulfilling prophecy.

Chapter 13:

Contribute To Society In A Meaningful Way

Today we are going to talk about how and why you should do work that contributes to society in a meaningful way. And the benefits that it can bring to all aspects of your life, be it psychological, sociological, or physical.

Why do I feel that this topic is of importance that I should highlight it in today's episode? Well because if there is one thing i have noticed about my salaried friend workers around me, I do feel that they lack a bigger vision and purpose for their life. And i feel that there is a sense that the end goal of their work is not to the benefit of their own personal growth, but of the $ sign at the end. And this motivation to work towards a 5 figure pay check is one that ultimately brings not much joy and meaning to one's life.

The many friends that I have interviewed have told me repeatedly that these jobs are merely a means to an end. That it's a routine that they have pretty much resigned themselves to sustain a lifestyle that they feel is good enough for them. This mentality has gotten me to question the culture of whether a monetary goal is truly sufficient in making one truly happy. Yes to an extent, money can bring about freedom which would free up time for one to pursue their passions in life, but for most, this race towards $10k just feels futile.

I would argue that only when you know what to do with freedom of time, and that is to serve a purpose greater than your own selfish needs, can you truly have a meaningful time on this earth.

The greatest entrepreneurs today make their millions not by chasing the money per se, but rather by finding problems that they can solve. They find a gap in society, a need that needs to be filled, and invent a novel solution to a problem that aims to address those holes. Think Jeff Bezos, Steve Jobs, Elon Musk, Mark Zuckerberg. These billionaires have their customers and consumers in mind when they set out to create their mega companies that have largely dominated our world today.

Now I am not saying you need to be doing these crazy big deals to live a happy life, but i believe that everyone has an ability to start somewhere, to start small in our community. If you have no desire for entrepreneurship and are contented with being a salaried worker, that is absolutely perfect. However you can consider doing some volunteer work, and working with a community that can better the lives of someone out there even if it just by a little bit. I guarantee that these selfless acts of giving your time to help someone out in your unique way will reward you with a feeling that money just can't buy.

If you feel like you can do more, you can dedicate more of your time to a particular cause that resonates with you, that you will not feel like a chore to serve. A cause that strikes your heart and soul that makes you want to go back so that you can give more and do more.

Maybe this cause will be something you might end up dedicating your life to, you never know. But I do know that chasing money and dedicating your life to making money will never make you happy. Invest in others, invest in their spirit, invest in doing good for society will be infinitely more worthy of your time and energy.

I challenge you today to see in what areas can you contribute to society and do good for others. I believe that you will not only feel purpose, but it will help sustain you in your career and work as well, giving you a fresh perspective on what life is really all about.

Chapter 14:

6 Ways To Adopt A Better Lifestyle For Long-Term Success

A good lifestyle leads to a good life. The important choices we make throughout our lives impact our future in numerous ways. The need to make ourselves better in every aspect of life and the primary ability to perform such a routine can be a lifestyle. There is no proper way to live written in a book; however, through our shared knowledge and our comprehension, we can shape a lifestyle that can be beneficial and exciting at the same time. Though there is no doubt that falling into a specific routine can be difficult but, maintaining a proper state is more critical for a successful life.

For long-term success, a good lifestyle is a priority. Almost everything we do in our lives directly or indirectly involves our future self. So, a man needs to become habitual of such things that can profit him in every way possible. To visualize a better you, You need to configure just about everything around you. And to change all the habits that may make you feel lagging. The most common feature of a better lifestyle for long-term success is determination.

1. **Change In Pattern Of Your Life**

It is good to shape a pattern of living from the start and forming good habits, engaging yourself in profitable practice, and choosing a healthier custom. It feels impossible to change something you have already been habitual of, but willpower is the key. With some motivation and dedication, you can change yourself into a better version of yourself. You are choosing what might be suitable for you and staying determined on that thought. The first step is to let go of harmful things slowly because letting go of habits and patterns that you are used to can be challenging. After some, sometime you will notice yourself letting go of things more easily.

2. Take Your Time

Time is an essential factor when it comes to forming a lifestyle for a successful life. Time can seem to slow through the process, making us think that it may have been stopped in our most difficult moments. Similarly, making us feel it goes flying by when our life is relaxed and at ease. Time never stops for anyone. It is crucial to make sure we make most of our time and consume it in gaining more knowledge and power. Take time to inform your lifestyle, but not more than required. We are taking things at a moderate pace so you can both enjoy life and do work.

3. Don't Always Expect Things To Go Your Way

As much as we humans like to get our hopes high, we can't always expect things to go our way. Even things we have worked hard for can sometimes go downhill. It is at times overconfidence, but sometimes it can be pure bad luck. We can't get disheartened by something that was not meant to go a specific way. Don't expect perfection in all the work you do. Staying patient is the walk towards the reward. And making the best out of the worst can be the only way to get yourself going.

4. Don't Be Afraid To Ask For Help

It is human nature to ask each other for help now and then. If it comes to this point, don't be afraid to ask for help yourself. Ask someone superior to aid you on matters you find difficult. Don't hesitate to ask your inferiors who might have more knowledge than you in some certain customs. Help them, too, if needed. Ask them to assist you out on points, but never make them do the whole project. Don't make someone do something you wouldn't do yourself.

5. Be Prompt In Everything

Lagging behind your work can be the worst possible habit you could raise. Make yourself punctual in every aspect. Make sure you are on time everywhere. Either it's to wake up in the morning or to go to a meeting. Laziness can never be proven good for you or your dream towards a prosperous lifestyle. Respect time, and it shall respect you. Show your colleges that they can depend on you to show up on time and take responsibility for work. You would rather wait than making others wait for you. That will show you seriousness toward your business.

6. Keep A Positive Attitude

Keeping a positive attitude can lead to a positive lifestyle. Be happy with yourself in every context, and make sure that everything you do has your complete confidence. Be thankful to all who surround you. Keep a positive attitude, whether it be a home or office. Speak with your superiors with respect and make yourself approachable around inferiors. Your positive mindset can affect others in a way too. They will become more inclined towards you, and they can easily suggest you help someone.

Conclusion

Just about everything in your life affects your future in a way or other, so make sure that you do all you can to make yourself worth the praise. Keep your lifestyle simple but effective. Try to do as much as possible for yourself and make time to relax as well. For long-term success, willpower is the most important; make sure you have it. Keep your headlight and calm for the upcoming difficulties and prepare yourself to face almost everything life throws at you.

Chapter 15:

How To Find Your Passion

Today we're going to talk about a topic that i think many of you are interested to know about. And that is how to find your passion.

For many of us, the realities of work and obligations means that we end up doing something we dislike for the money in the hopes that it might buy us some happiness. That sometimes we stop following our passion because maybe it does not exactly pay very well. And that is a fair decision to make.

But today, i hope to be able to help you follow at least one passion project at any point in your life in the hopes that it might help elevate your spirits, give your life more meaning, and help you live each day with a renewed drive and purpose.

You see, the world can be very dull if we chase something that we actually don't really feel attracted to. For example, when we are forced to do something out of sheer dread day in and day out, it will suck the living soul out of us and we will tend to fall into the trap of running an endless wheel with no hope in sight. When we chase material things for example, money or luxury products, we sell our soul to a job that pays well physically but not emotionally and spiritually. As a human being, we have traded our very essence and time, for a piece of paper or digital currency that serves no purpose than to enrich us externally. While it might feel good to be living comfortably, past a certain threshold, there is a point of diminishing returns. And more money just doesn't bring you that much joy anymore.

Yes you may have the fanciest, car, house, and whatever physical possessions you have. But how many of you have heard stories of people who have a lot of money but end up depressed, or end up blowing it all away because they can never spend enough to satisfy their cravings for physical goods and services. What these people lacked in emotional growth, they tried to overcompensate with money. And as their inner self gets emptier and emptier, they themselves get poorer and poorer as well.

On the flip side, many would argue that passion is overrated. That passion is nothing but some imaginary thing that we tell ourselves we need to have in order to be happy. But i am here to argue that you do not need to make passion your career in order to be happy.

You see, passion is an aspiration, passion is something that excites you, passion is something that you would do even if it does not pay a single cent. That you would gladly trade your time readily for even if it meant u weren't getting anything monetary in return. Because this passion unlocks something within you that cannot be explained with being awarded physical prizes. It is the feeling that you are truly alive and happy, you are so incredibly grateful and thankful to be doing at that very moment in time, that nothing else mattered, not even sleep.

To me, and I hope you will see this too, that passion can be anything you make it out to be. It can be something as simple as a passion for singing, a passion for creating music, a passion for helping others, passion for supporting your family, passion for starting a family, passion for doing charity work, passion for supporting a cause monetarily, or even a passion for living life to the fullest and being grateful each day.

For some lucky ones, they have managed to marry their passion with their career. They have somehow made their favourite thing to do their job, and it fulfills them each day. To those people, i congratulate you and envy you.

But for the rest of us, our passion can be something we align our soul with as long as it fulfils us as well. If we have multiple mouths to feed, we can make our passion as being the breadwinner to provide for our family if it brings us joy to see them happy. If we have a day job that we hate but can't let go off for whatever reasons, we can have a passion for helping others, to use the income that we make to better the lives of others.

And for those who have free time but are not sure what to do with it, to just simply start exploring different interests and see what hobbies you resonate with. You may never know what you might discover if you did a little digging.

What I have come to realize is that passions rarely stay the same. They change as we change, they evolve over time just as we grow. And many of the passions we had when we were younger, we might outgrow them when we hit a certain age. As our priorities in life change, our passions follow along.

In my opinion, you do not need to make your passion your career in order to be truly happy.. I believe that all you need is to have at least 1 passion project at any given point of time in your life to sustain you emotionally and spiritually. Something that you can look forward to on your off days, in your time away from work, that you can pour all your time and energy into willingly without feeling that you have wasted any second. And who knows, you might feel so strongly about that passion project that you might even decide to make it your career some day. The thing is you never really know. Life is mysterious like that.

All I do know is that chasing money for the wrong reasons will never net u happiness. But having a passion, whatever it may be, will keep you grounded and alive.

So I challenge each and everyone of you today to look into your current life, and see there are any bright spots that you have neglected that you could revive and make it your passion project. Remember that passion can be anything you make out to be as long as you derive fulfilment and happiness from it. Helpfully one that isnt material or monetary.

Chapter 16:

10 Habits of Joe Biden

There is a proclamation that portrays leaders as people who meet their times. Probably the contrary appears true for US president Joe Biden. Time has met the man!

Since its inception, President Joe Biden's political career has been distinguished by a seismic lurch, from setbacks to triumphs. Biden has served in the United States Senate for 36 years and as Vice President for two terms under Barack Obama's administration. All along, he became the ultimate political ally and the nation's unofficial top consoler.

His third run for the White House was unfolding just as expected: a front running falls into oblivion. Then came Super Tuesday. What can you grasp from the man whose fate just intervened for greatness?

Here are 10 habits of Joe Biden.

1. He Works With Objectives

According to Matthew Crayne, an organizational psychologist, and professor, one of Joe Biden's strengths in handling the Covid-19 vaccine rollout is that he has maintained a clear set of objectives that are easily communicated and understood. Essentially, clear objectives will disclose your program's success and setbacks.

2. Don't Bluff

Given the heated relationship between the United States and Russia over the years-from Crimea to Syria to election involvement to ransomware-you might think Biden's meeting with Russian President Putin earlier this year was a bluff. Truth is, he went to Geneva that early in his presidency with specific goals in mind; to establish the terms of their relationship.

3. A Waver? No

Biden hasn't wavered in his vision for the future, and he continually emphasizes that progress is being made, but the mission isn't finished. As a leader, employing this habit in your strategies will help impart a sense of accomplishment and urgency into the population, both of which are vital in driving long-term collective action.

4. He Embraces His Mistakes

Joe Biden's past journey to the White House was rocky, from allegations tarnishing his academic credentials to controversy over handling Clarence Thomas Supreme court case. However, he didn't derail in admitting his mistakes, a character that could later rank him as the most trustworthy politician according to a 2015 CBS News/New York Times survey. Embracing your mistakes is a crucial foundation of your every worthwhile goal.

5. Sets Good Examples

As a leader, your work is to influence those you lead by acting accordingly. While fighting the spread of the Corona Virus, President Biden has leveraged his office's status and influence to conduct symbolic gestures. Wearing a mask during public appearances and publicly getting his dose of the vaccination. This may appear apparent and expected, but still is influential for collective action.

6. Get Stuff Done

The only thing that should matter is the outcome, and so, for example, if you recall when President Obama said, Joe's going to do the Recovery Act and its Sheriff Joe, and nobody messes with me. The guys in the House and Senate applauded, saying, "Yeah, that's Joe. And we like Joe like that."

7. Empathy Defines Him

As a leader, how you respond to adversity is a guide to your character. Biden is moved by his personal tragedies in consoling the masses. His impassionate statement the day before his inauguration to the relatives of the 400,000 Americans killed by Covid-19 says it all.

8. Actions Are Better

Holding back from acting prevents you from exploring your capabilities and abilities. President Biden's choice to meet with Russian President showed that he was a man of actions. That is, he attended the meeting in good faith, seeking to pave the way for normative accords, which in turn could provide Americans and their allies with a way forward.

9. Be Humble

Under Trump's leadership, the US devolved into a dangerous place for its profound racial gap. Biden's seeming humility, hard-won and life-learned, lends itself well to reconciling the problem. More often, it is your hard humbling that will assist you in reaching a point where you can make the necessary changes.

10. You're Not Bigger Than Your Role

The job of a leader encompasses more than just you. It's never about you; it's always about the people, the nation. Power is something you must acquire, and not given to you by your role. The best leaders like President Biden have an unrivaled desire to lead others in a cause greater than themselves.

Conclusion

The measure of a person is not how frequently he falls but how swiftly he gets up. Failure is unavoidable at some times, but quitting is inexcusable. With all of its ups and downs, Biden's habits will teach you some essential leadership lessons.

Chapter 17:

Happy People Stay Grateful For Everything They Have

A lot of us will have different answers to this simple question, "what are you grateful for today?" It could differ from as simple as getting out of bed to achieving that huge task you had your mind on for a while. Gratitude is the emotion we feel when we tend to notice and appreciate the good things that have come into our lives. Some people feel grateful for even the tiniest things, while others don't even if they achieve more than they have wished for. Most of the time, people who will be thankful still feel negative emotions, but they tend to shift their focus from all the bad things in their lives to the good ones.

Research has shown that teenagers and adults who feel more grateful than others are also happier, get better grades, have better friends, get more opportunities, have fewer illnesses and pain, have more energy, and tend to sleep better. The link of practicing gratitude to achieve happiness is through a path that we commonly call the "cognitive pathway." The words "cognitive" and "cognition" are used by scientists to talk about thinking; if we don't think about the good things in our life, we would not feel grateful.

Most situations that happen in our lives are neither all good nor all bad. It is on us how we trick our minds and interpret the effect of the situation on our lives. One of the thinking habits is called a "positive interpretation bias," which means that we are most likely to interpret a neutral or negative situation positively. On the contrary, some people tend to ignore all the positive aspects of their problems and finds excuses and reasons to focus more on the negativity.

Studies also show that people who practice gratitude remember more good memories than bad ones. A more grateful person tends to encode more positive memories and keeps out the negative ones. They are also tended to be healthier and are sick less often. This is because they worry less about all the wrong things and focus more on the positive stuff they had achieved throughout the days. They keep their negative emotions to a minimum. A study showed that people who felt more grateful also had increased brain activity essential for both emotional and cognitive processes.

Happiness and gratitude go hand in hand and can be practiced in a lot of different ways. One way is to write a list of all the good things that have happened to you every day and go through it before you sleep. Another way is to send some love to your close ones, thanking and appreciating all that they have done for you. While it is essential to practice gratitude every day, it is also important to know that the bad things shouldn't be ignored. In fact, the real test of gratitude is how we act on the situations when they don't go as per our plans. We don't always need to be happy to be grateful, but gratitude indeed leads to greater happiness.

Chapter 18:

How to Embrace Adventure to Change Your Life

Human beings are creatures of habit. This can be a good thing, as the habits we form can allow us to autopilot through the more tedious aspects of life. But as the years go by, many of us put not only a few habits but our *entire lives* on autopilot. And when we do so, we develop a problem of *sameness*. We stagnate, and our once-steady supply of new experiences dries up.

So what's the cost of this?

When we stop engaging in the new, we stop developing as people. We stop growing. And when we stop growing, the monotony and boredom set in, often felt in the form of a nagging feeling that something just isn't right in our lives. If that sounds like you, it might be time to break out of the habits causing you to stagnate. To help you do this, let's look at ways you can bring adventure back into your life.

You get up. You eat a lackluster breakfast. You rush to work. You get off at 6. You watch television for a few hours. You go to bed. You repeat. Sound familiar?

Sameness has a way of making us feel like monotony is normal. We stop living, begin merely existing, and—amazingly—we feel comfortable in that. But the simple act of shaking up your routine can open your eyes to the world of adventure that's always just outside your door.

Add a Third Space

What's a third place, you might ask? In short, it's one of the keys to adventure!

A third place is somewhere that is separate from your two most-visited social environments: work and home. It's the local coffee shop where you might go to work on your latest short story. It's the barbershop where you'd go to have a chat about the latest happenings in the neighborhood. It's the library you run for when you need a quiet moment of contemplation.

Unlike someone's first place, which is the home, and the second place, which is work, the third place tends to blend community life and self-expression. It's a place where, unlike at work, you can relax and be yourself, and unlike at home, you're pushed to explore new possibilities, often through social interaction. Finding your third place, whatever that might be, is essential to breaking up the monotony of life and finding new adventures and new people. Start scouring your neighborhood for one today!

Choose a New Path

It's the experience of life that we remember the most, and it is the memories of these experiences make us happiest in old age. Regret is built upon a life of sameness—don't let that be you.

Change your habits. Change your life. Find adventure.

Now, get out there and do it.

Chapter 19:

<u>10 Habits of Kobe Bryant</u>

Throughout 20 seasons, the late Kobe Bryant earned a reputation as the greatest basketball player of all time with the Los Angeles Lakers. The six-foot-six shooting guard dominated the court in NBA history, winning five NBA titles, a record of 18 consecutive All-Star Game selections, four All-Star Game MVP Awards, and the Academy Award for Best Animated Short Film, "Dear Basketball."

Bryant's off-court legacy was similarly outstanding, with record earnings for an NBA player, winning investments, and a lucrative shoe deal that increased his net worth to more than $600 million. He was also renowned for his strong work ethic. Highly applauded, you'll find endless stories on his 20-year career work ethics from his teammates, competitors, coaches, and other acquaintances.

Here are 10 Kobe Bryant's habits.

1. His Work Ethics

Kobe Bryant was well-known for having a solid work ethic. If he ever lost a game, he could figure out why and spend extra time improving. Losing a shot for Kobe meant training for hours and days until he couldn't miss it anymore. He was going to train so hard that you wouldn't beat him.

2. Become Obsessive

Kobe not only obsessed on basketball, but also dedicated his energy on becoming the best in every manner. "If you want to be exceptional at something, you have to obsess over it," he once said. That's precisely the mind set you need if you want to be the best in your field. Embrace your obsession, fall in love with the process, and use it to reach heights that others cannot.

3. Mamba Attitude

Kobe was determined to be one of the greatest basketballers at only 13 years of age. He said in an interview that he was inspired by great players like Michael Jordan and Magic Jordan. He would watch them play and wonder, "Can I get to that level?" "i don't know," he could say, "but let's find out." Whether you're starting a business, becoming a great athlete, learning a new skill, or forming a new habit, modelling your habits after someone who has already succeeded will save you the most time and money in the long run.

4. Compete Against Yourself

When you compete with yourself, you put others in the position to keep up with you. Kobe never had this problem because he fought within him to be the type of athlete who could win more after winning his first championship. Throughout his career, he progressed from being the No. 8 Kobe who wanted to win to the No. 24 Kobe who needed to be a leader and a better teammate.

5. Embracing New Abilities

After Kobe retired from sports in 2016, his next focus was on finding ways to inspire the world through diverse stories, characters, and leadership. He pushed and founded multimedia production company Granity Studios, which is 2018, lead to his Academy Award- a Sports Emmy and an Annie Award for his short animated film Dear Basketball. Embracing new skills will keep your legacy going and diversify your abilities in different walks of life.

6. Leaders develop leaders

"I enjoyed testing people and making them uncomfortable," Kobe once said. "That is what leads to introspection, which leads to improvement. I guess you could say I challenged them to be their best selves." On the court, Kobe was a strong, albeit contentious, leader for his team.

7. Handling the Pressure is Everything

When you're under pressure, you're forced to make critical choices and decisions. Sometimes, you'll make the wrong decisions, but that what keeps you going strong. When Kobe was playing against the Utah Jazz at 18 years, he missed a shot which led to his team losing the game. This had him working on the shot during the entire off-season.

8. Perseverance

Kobe's success was as a result of sticking to his process through perseverance. He was determined not to give in to anyone or anything that pushed him backwards. Your strength to keep moving will eventually payoff.

9. Failure Begets Growth

Failure is only ideal when you keep learning. In an interview, Kobe mentioned being an 11-year-old basketball player who played in a summer league for an entire season without scoring a single point! Really?! So he had to work extra for the following ten months to become a better shot and learn how to score.

10. Passion Is Everything

It's undeniable that Kobe had a strong love and enthusiasm for basketball. His passion for basketball, his work ethic, and competitiveness helped him become a five-time champion. When you sincerely love your craft, and put more into it, you will always rise against the odds to achieve success.

Conclusion

Although Bryant was an exceptional talent, his success was a product of an intense, obsessive work ethic. Bryant's desire to be the best was evident in almost every aspect of his life.

Chapter 20:

7 Ways To Cultivate Emotions That Will Lead You To Greatness

Billions of men and women have walked the earth but only a handful have made their names engraved in history forever. These handful of people have achieved 'greatness' owing to their outstanding work, their passion and their character.

Now, greatness doesn't come overnight—greatness is not something you can just reach out and grab. Greatness is the result of how you have lived your entire life and what you have achieved in your lifetime. Against all your given circumstances, how impactful your life has been in this world, how much value you have given to the people around you, how much difference your presence has made in history counts towards how great you are. However, even though human greatness is subjective, people who are different and who have stood out from everyone else in a particular matter are perceived as great.

However, cultivating greatness in life asks for a 'great' deal of effort and all kinds of human effort are influenced by human emotions. So it's safe to say that greatness is, in fact, controlled by our emotions. Having said that, let's see what emotions are associated with greatness and how to cultivate them in real life:

1. Foster Gratitude

You cannot commence your journey towards greatness without being grateful first. That's right, being satisfied with what you already have in life and expressing due gratitude towards it will be your first step towards greatness. Being in a gratified emotional state at most times (if not all) will enhance your mental stability which will consequently help you perceive life in a different—or better point of view. This enhanced perception of life will remove your stresses and allow you to develop beyond the mediocrity of life and towards greatness.

2. Be As Curious As Child

Childhood is the time when a person starts to learn whatever that is around them. A child never stops questioning, a child never runs away from what they have to face. They just deal with things head on. Such kind of eagerness for life is something that most of us lose at the expense of time. As we grow up—as we know more, our interest keeps diminishing. We stop questioning anymore and accept what is. Eventually, we become entrapped into the ordinary. On the contrary, if we greet everything in life with bold eagerness, we expose ourselves to opportunities. And opportunities lead to greatness.

3. Ignite Your Passion

Passion has become a cliché term in any discussion related to achievements and life. Nevertheless, there is no way of denying the role of passion in driving your life force. Your ultimate zeal and fervor towards what you want in life is what distinguishes you to be great. Because admittedly, many people may want the same thing in life but how bad they want it—the intensity of wanting something is what drives people to stand out from the rest and win it over.

4. Become As Persistent As A Mountain

There are two types of great people on earth—1) Those who are born great and 2) Those who persistently work hard to become great. If you're reading this article, you probably belong to the later criteria. Being such, your determination is a key factor towards becoming great. Let nothing obstruct you—remain as firm as a mountain through all thick and thin. That kind of determination is what makes extraordinary out of the ordinary.

5. Develop Adaptability

As I have mentioned earlier, unless you are born great, your journey towards greatness will be an extremely demanding one. You will have to embrace great lengths beyond your comfort. In order to come out successful in such a journey, make sure that you become flexible to unexpected changes in your surroundings. Again, making yourself adaptable first in another journey in itself. You can't make yourself fit in adverse situations immediately. Adaptability or flexibility is cultivated prudently, with time, exposing yourself to adversities, little by little.

6. Confidence Is Key

Road to greatness often means that you have to tread a path that is discouraged by most. It's obvious—by definition, everybody cannot be great. People will most likely advise against you when you aspire something out of the ordinary. Some will even present logical explanations against you;especially your close ones. But nothing should waver your faith. You must remain boldly confident towards what you're pursuing. Only you can bring your greatness. Believe that.

7. Sense of Fulfilment Through Contributions

Honestly, there can be no greater feeling than what you'd feel after your presence has made a real impact on this world. If not, what else do we live for? Having contributed to the world and the people around you; this is the purpose of life. All the big and small contributions you make give meaning to your existence. It connects you to others, man and animal alike. It fulfills your purpose as a human being. We live for this sense of fulfillment and so, become a serial contributor. Create in yourself a greed for this feeling. At the end of the day, those who benefit from your contributions will revere you as great. No amount of success can be compared with this kind of greatness. So, never miss the opportunity of doing a good deed, no matter how minuscule or enormous.

In conclusion, these emotions don't come spontaneously. You have to create these emotions, cultivate them. And to cultivate these emotions, you must first understand yourself and your goals. With your eye on the prize, you have to create these emotions in you which will pave the path to your greatness. Gratitude, curiosity, passion, persistence, adaptability and fulfillment—each has its own weight and with all the emotions at play, nothing can stop you from becoming great in the truest form.

Chapter 21:

Do More of What Already Works

In 2004, nine hospitals in Michigan began implementing a new procedure in their intensive care units (I.C.U.). Almost overnight, healthcare professionals were stunned by its success.

Three months after it began, the procedure had cut the infection rate of I.C.U. Patients by sixty-six percent. Within 18 months, this one method had saved 75 million dollars in healthcare expenses. Best of all, this single intervention saved the lives of more than 1,500 people in just a year and a half. The strategy was immediately published in a blockbuster paper for the New England Journal of Medicine.

This medical miracle was also simpler than you could ever imagine. It was a checklist.

This five-step checklist was the simple solution that Michigan hospitals used to save 1,500 lives. Think about that for a moment. There were no technical innovations. There were no pharmaceutical discoveries or cutting-edge procedures. The physicians just stopped skipping steps. They implemented the answers they already had on a more consistent basis.

New Solutions vs. Old Solutions

We tend to undervalue answers that we have already discovered. We underutilize old solutions—even best practices—because they seem like something we have already considered.

Here's the problem: *"Everybody already knows that"* is very different from *"Everybody already does that."* Just because a solution is known doesn't mean it is utilized.

Even more critical, just because a solution is implemented occasionally doesn't mean it is implemented consistently. Every physician knew the five steps on Peter Pronovost's checklist, but very few did all five steps flawlessly each time.

We assume that new solutions are needed to make real progress, but that isn't always the case. This pattern is just as present in our personal lives as it is in corporations and governments. We waste the resources and ideas at our fingertips because they don't seem new and exciting.

There are many examples of behaviors, big and small, that have the opportunity to drive progress in our lives if we just did them with more consistency—flossing every day—never missing workouts. Performing fundamental business tasks each day, not just when you have time—apologizing more often. Writing Thank You notes each week.

Of course, these answers are boring. Mastering the fundamentals isn't sexy, but it works. No matter what task you are working on, a simple checklist of steps you can follow right now—fundamentals that you have known about for years—can immediately yield results if you just practice them more consistently.

Progress often hides behind boring solutions and underused insights. You don't need more information. You don't need a better strategy. You just need to do more of what already works.

Chapter 22:

8 Tips to Boost Your Productivity with Superfoods

You've probably heard how the most successful people in the world look for productivity boosters in the form of exercise and a strict schedule. Did you also know that the foods you eat could significantly impact your brain and motivation? According to the World Health Organization, the right foods can increase brainpower, motivation, and overall productivity by up to 20 percent.

This finding is linked most directly with those who work in office buildings and other work settings with few nutritious dining and snacking options, but it still applies to the entire workforce to some degree. All in all, the foods we eat have a profound impact on our work output. If you've noticed you've been a little more sluggish at work lately, consider adding these superfoods to your daily diet.

1. Salmon

Fatty fishes are excellent for promoting productivity, and salmon is one of the best of them all. Salmon has high omega-3 fatty acids content, which is particularly useful for improving memory and mental performance, particularly helping depression, which can be the utter antithesis of productivity.

According to an article from Livestrong.com, "An eight-week study involving 28 patients with major depression found that those taking omega-3s in addition to usual treatment had significantly decreased depression scores compared to those taking placebo and the usual treatment." The article recommends either eating more salmon or taking a fish oil supplement to achieve a similar result.

2. Berries

Antioxidant-rich foods, like berries, are excellent for increasing memory, improving memory function in the workplace, and preventing Alzheimer's and Parkinson's in the future. As a general rule of thumb, the darker the berry is, the higher its antioxidant property, which means it has more productivity-boosting ingredients.

3. Green Tea

Green tea is a natural energy enhancer without the negative side effects of other energy-fabricating ingredients. One of the most effective types of green tea for energy production is Matcha, which has become extremely popular over the last few years, particularly in New York City.

"Matcha is unique because the entire green tea leaf is ground into a fine powder and consumed, unlike other teas where leaves are submerged into hot water to steep," says an article from NYHRC, a New York health club. "Ingesting the whole leaf provides fiber and polyphenols, a family of powerful antioxidants."

4. Dark Chocolate

Who says all sugar is bad for you? Dark chocolate is excellent for both satisfying that sweet little tooth and improving overall focus. The candy's caffeine content helps you feel more energetic and focused on the tasks at hand. It also contains magnesium, which is a natural stress reliever. For a guilt-free, energy-boosting treat, break off just a quarter of a bar for a great-tasting energy enhancement.

5. Nuts

You should reach for a handful of nuts for a couple of reasons. For starters, nuts are an excellent source of protein and natural fat that your body needs to be healthy. Secondly, they are an antioxidant, vitamin E, and amino acid-rich food, which means they'll give your body the natural increase in memory and brain performance you need to make it through the day. Almonds and walnuts contain some of the best ingredients for brainpower.

6. Avocados

The secret to productivity is keeping consistent blood flowing around the heart and through the brain. Avocados are a natural stimulant for that very reason. According to WebMD, an avocado a day "enhances blood flow, offering a simple, tasty way to fire up brain cells." This is another healthy fat for your body that tastes delicious and improves your overall focus.

7. Water

This last one may not be food, but it's still enormously useful for enhancing productivity in the workplace. Since your body is made up of more than 70 percent water, every function in the body depends on water to work smoothly. Your water stores slowly deplete throughout the day, and if you don't drink enough water to replenish the lost liquid, your brain and other functions suffer the consequences.

Devoting the energy to drinking at least eight glasses of water a day will give your brain the power it needs to be more focused and think more clearly and quickly.

8. Bananas

Glucose in the body equals energy, and bananas are some of the best resources for that energy-inducing ingredient. A single banana holds the daily amount of glucose your body needs, and it's a much healthier way to get it than excessive carbs and cane sugars. It's also extremely filling, which means that you'll be able to focus better between meals if you snack on this rather than something less filling.

Chapter 23:

<u>5 Habits of Good Speech Delivery</u>

Speech delivery is a hot topic amongst many people with opinions divided on what to or what not to do. Everyone has their struggle in speech delivery; some are shy, others are bold but lack the material content to deliver while another group cannot hold a coherent conversation altogether with strangers.

Here are five fundamental habits of good speech delivery:

1. Understand Your Audience

Whenever given the chance to address an audience, it is imperative to understand the demographic constitution of your audience. Their age, social and political class contributes heavily to how they will perceive your speech.

The manner one can deliver a speech to a graduation class at a university is entirely different from how the same speech can be given to entrepreneurs considering the mindset and life priorities of these two groups.

When you have a thorough understanding of your audience, your art of public speaking and speech delivery will improve because your audience will relate well.

2. Read The Mood and Setting of Your Audience

The diction and language of your speech are variables of the prevailing mood of the audience. How can you relate with them if you are blind to their present mood (excitement or somberness) or the setting (high or low temperatures)?

The wearer of a shoe knows where it pinches. As a speaker, you should be flexible to allow your audience to follow your speech in their most comfortable state. If the weather is hot, allow them to open windows and air ventilation. If they are in a bad mood, make them understand that you feel their plight.

Be the bigger person in the room and accommodate everyone. It will earn you respect and your speech will be well received.

3. Understand the Theme of The Speech

This is the core subject matter of the speech. Every speech aims to pass a specific message to its recipients. Under no circumstances should the theme be lost to any other interest. If it does, the speech would be meaningless and a waste of time.

The onus is upon the deliverer of the speech to stick to the theme and neither alter nor dilute the message therein. He/she should first understand it to be able to convey the same to the audience. The speaker should not have any malice or prejudice to any section of the audience. They should have clean hands.

It is paramount to understand that the audience is not ignorant of the theme of the speech. When you disappoint their expectations, you would have lost their participation and some of them may leave the meeting in progress. The chance to deliver a speech does not render the rest of the audience is inferior to the speaker.

4. Be Bold

Boldness is the courage to speak fearlessly without mincing your words. Bold speakers are rare to come by and when they do, their audience becomes thrilled by their exuberance of knowledge. The content of a speech could be great but when a coward delivers it, the theme is lost.

Boldness captures the attention of the audience. They expect the best from a bold speaker. The best orators of our time speak so powerfully that one cannot ignore them. The 44th president of the United States is a perfect example of how he boldly delivered his speeches and commanded respect across the globe.

A bold speaker does not bore his/her audience and they are more likely to remember a speech that they delivered compared to those of timid speakers. Fortune favors the bold.

5. Engage Your Audience

It is important to bring onboard your audience when you are delivering a speech. They will feel included and it will be more of a conversation than a talk down. When an audience actively participates in the delivery of a speech, it is more likely they will remember it.

As a speaker, maintain eye contact with the audience. This will create a connection with them and remove the notion that you are afraid of them. From time to time in your speech, rope them in to answer a relatable question. An audience expectant of engagement from its speaker will be more attentive.

A speech is not a monologue. It is an interaction between the speaker and his/her audience. When a speaker monopolizes a speech, it becomes boring and easily forgettable. It may further come out as a show-off rather than a genuine speech of a particular theme.

These are the five key habits if you want to maximize the delivery of your speech.

Chapter 24:

Saying Yes To Things

Today we're going to talk about why saying yes can be a great thing for you and why you should do so especially in social invites.

Life you see is a funny thing. As humans, we tend to see things one dimensionally. And we tend to think that we have a long life ahead of us. We tend to take things for granted. We think we will have time to really have fun and relax after we have retired and so we should spend all our efforts and energy into building a career right now, prioritising it above all else. When faced with a choice between work and play, sometimes many of us, including myself choose work over social invites.

There were periods in my life that i routinely chose work over events that it became such a habit to say no. Especially as an entrepreneur, the interaction between colleagues or being in social events is almost reduced to zero. It became very easy and comfortable to live in this bubble where my one and only priority in life is to work work work. 24 hours, 7 days a week. Of course, in reality a lot of time was wasted on social media and Netflix, but u know, at least i could sort of pretend that i was kind of working all day. And I was sort of being productive and sort of working towards my goals rather than "wasting time on social events". That was what I told myself anyway.

But life does not work that way. As I prioritised work over all else, soon all the social invite offers started drying up. My constant "nos" were becoming evident to my social circle and I was being listed as perpetually unavailable or uninterested in vesting time or energy into any friendships or relationships. And as i retreated deeper and deeper into this black hole of "working remotely" i found myself completely isolated from new experiences and meeting new people, or even completely stopped being involved in any of my friend's lives.

I've successfully written myself out of life and I found myself all alone in it.

Instead of investing time into any meaningful relationships, I found that my closest friends were my laptop, tablet, phone, and television. Technology became my primary way of interacting with the world. And I felt connected, yet empty. I was always plugged in to wifi, but i lived my life through a screen instead of my own two eyes. My work and bedroom became a shell of a home that I spent almost all my time, and life just became sort of pointless. And I just felt very alone.

As I started to feel more and more like something was missing, I couldn't quite make out what it was that led me to this feeling. I simply though to myself, hey I'm prioritising work and my career, making money is what the internet tells me I should do, and not having a life is simply part of the price you have to pay... so why am I so incredibly unhappy?

As it turns out, as I hope many of you have already figured out at this point, that life isn't really just about becoming successful financially.

While buying a house, getting a car, and all that good stuff is definitely something that we should strive towards, we should not do so at the expense of our friends. That instead of saying no to them, we should start saying yes, at least once in a while. We need to signal to our friends that hey, yes even though I'm very busy, but I will make an effort to carve out time for you, so that you know I still value you in my life and that you are still a priority.

We need to show our friends that while Monday may not work for us, that I have an opening maybe 2 weeks later if you're still down. That we are still available to grow this friendship.

I came to a point in my life where I knew something had to change. As I started examining my life and the decisions I had made along the way with regards to my career, I knew that what I did wrong was saying no WAAAAAY too often. As I tried to recall when was the last time I actually when I went out with someone other than my one and only BFF, I simply could not. Of the years that went by, I had either said that I was too busy, or even on the off chances that I actually agreed to some sort of meetup, I had the habit of bailing last minute on lunch and dinner appointments with friends. And I never realized that i had such a terrible reputation of being a flaker until I started doing some serious accounting of my life. I had become someone that I absolutely detested without even realising it. I have had people bail on me at the very last minute before, and I hated that feeling. And whenever someone did that to me, I generally found it difficult to ask them out again because I felt that they weren't really that interested in meeting me anyway. That they didn't even bother to reschedule the appointment. And little did I know, I was becoming that very same person and doing the very thing that I hate to my friends. It is no wonder that I started dropping friends like flies with my terrible actions.

As I came to this revelation, I started panicking. It was as if a truck had hit me so hard that I felt that I was in a terrible accident. That how did I let myself get banged up to that extent?

I started scrolling through my contact lists, trying to find friends that might still want to hang out with me. I realized that my WhatsApp was basically dry as a desert, and my calendar was just work for the last 3 years straight with no meaningful highlights, no social events worth noting.

It was at this point that I knew I had made a huge mistake and I needed to change course immediately. Salvaging friendships and prioritising social activities went to the top of my list.

I started creating a list of friends that I had remotely any connection to in the last 5 years and I started asking them out one by one. Some of my friends who i had asked out may not know this, but at that point in my life, i felt pretty desperate and alone and I hung on to every meeting as if my life depended on it. Whilst I did manage to make some appointments and met up with some of them. I soon realized that the damage had been done. That my friends had clearly moved on without me... they had formed their own friends at work and elsewhere, and I was not at all that important to have anymore. It was too little too late at that point and there was not much I could do about it. While I made multiple attempts to ask people out, I did not receive the same offers from people. It felt clearly like a one-way street and I felt that those people that I used to call friends, didn't really see me as one. You see growing a friendship takes time, sometimes years of consistent meetups before this person becomes indispensable in your life. Sharing unique experiences that allow your friends to see that you are truly vested in them and that you care about them and want to spend time with them. I simply did not give myself that chance to be integrated into someone's life in that same way, I did not invest that time to growing those friendships and I paid the price for it.

But I had to learn all these the hard way first before I can receive all the good that was about to come in the future.

In the next piece, I will show how i actually turned my life around by putting myself in positions where I will be exposed to more chances of social activity. And when saying yes became critical to growing a new social network for myself.

Chapter 25:

How to Value Being Alone

Some people are naturally happy alone. But for others, being solo is a challenge. If you fall into the latter group, there are ways to become more comfortable with being alone (yes, even if you're a hardcore extrovert).

Regardless of how you feel about being alone, building a good relationship with yourself is a worthy investment. After all, you *do* spend quite a bit of time with yourself, so you might as well learn to enjoy it.

Being alone isn't the same as being lonely.

Before getting into the different ways to find happiness in being alone, it's important to untangle these two concepts: being alone and being lonely. While there's some overlap between them, they're completely different concepts. Maybe you're a person who basks in solitude. You're not antisocial, friendless, or loveless. You're just quite content with alone time. You look forward to it. That's simply being alone, not being lonely.

On the other hand, maybe you're surrounded by family and friends but not relating beyond a surface level, which has you feeling empty and disconnected. Or maybe being alone just leaves you sad and longing for company. That's loneliness.

Short-term tips to get you started

These tips are aimed at helping you get the ball rolling. They might not transform your life overnight, but they can help you get more comfortable with being alone.

Some of them may be exactly what you needed to hear. Others may not make sense to you. Use them as stepping-stones. Add to them and shape them along the way to suit your lifestyle and personality.

1. Avoid comparing yourself to others.

This is easier said than done, but try to avoid comparing your social life to anyone else's. It's not the number of friends you have or the frequency of your social outings that matters. It's what works for you.

Remember, you have no way of knowing if someone with many friends and a stuffed social calendar is happy.

2. Take a step back from social media.

Social media isn't inherently bad or problematic, but if scrolling through your feeds makes you feel left out and stresses, take a few steps back. That feed doesn't tell the whole story. Not by a long shot.

You have no idea if those people are truly happy or just giving the impression that they are. Either way, it's no reflection on you. So, take a deep breath and put it in perspective.

Perform a test run and ban yourself from social media for 48 hours. If that makes a difference, try giving yourself a daily limit of 10 to 15 minutes and stick to it.

Don't be afraid to ask for help.

Sometimes, all the self-care, exercise, and gratitude lists in the world aren't enough to shake feelings of sadness or loneliness.

Consider reaching out to a therapist if:

- You're overly <u>stressed</u> and finding it difficult to cope.

- You have <u>symptoms of anxiety</u>.

- You have <u>symptoms of depression</u>.

You don't have to wait for a crisis point to get into <u>therapy</u>. Simply wanting to get better and spending time alone is a perfectly good reason to make an appointment.

Chapter 26:

<u>10 Habits of Warren Buffett</u>

Who does not know Warren Buffett? The multi-billionaire whose vast empire has built him a reputation nobody can dispute. Every businessperson aspires to be him someday.

These are the ten habits of Warren Buffett:

1. <u>He Is Progressive</u>

The man the world knows as wealthy was not born rich. At the age of twenty years, he had a paltry net worth of $20,000. Over the next seventy years, he has grown steadily to have a net worth of $103.8 billion. This is an indication of his progress over the years.

He is a testament to the saying hard work pays. Progress in his business empires is evident in the tax returns he pays to his country.

2. <u>He Is Patriotic</u>

Warren Buffet is a patriotic American citizen who duly remits taxes and abides by the law. In October 2016 during America's presidential elections, Mr. Buffett rose to the challenge of his rivals that he does not pay taxes. He came out clean and said that he has copies of all seventy-two of his returns and that he has paid federal income tax every year since 1944.

He also has no criminal record and no conviction of any crime whatsoever. By all measures and standards, he is a patriotic citizen.

3. He is Business-Oriented

A majority if not all the wealth Mr. Buffett has amassed is attributed to his businesses and not a salary. You cannot grow into the man he is today if you solely depend on your paycheck. You must be open-minded to venture into different businesses.

Warren Buffett runs his parent company, Berkshire Hathaway, which owns other companies like Duracell and Dairy Queen restaurant chain.

4. He is a Humble Person.

Mr. Warren Buffett is not a proud man despite being among the wealthiest people on the planet. If somebody else were in his position, he/she could have misused it. They could probably trample on the needy and the poor. This has never been Mr. Warren's character.

The soft-spoken man is humble in word and deed even when he is provoked into an argument as he was in 2016 regarding tax evasion claims by his rivals.

5. He Is Courageous

His courage in business is when he went against the norms of buying shares when no one was buying. He was buying when everybody else was selling. This is a bold move because there is uncertainty on the performance of the company issuing shares.

His courage also helped him overcome the fear of public speaking while he was young. Without it, he could not be the man he is today.

6. He Gives Free Advice

The most memorable advice that Mr. Buffett gave was to be fearful when others are greedy. He advises against following a popular opinion blindly. In investment, it pays to take a step back when other investors are buying shares greedily.

Mr. Buffett advises different groups of people whenever he gets the opportunity. He is not shy to share his wisdom and experience with the upcoming generation.

7. He is a Generous Philanthropist.

What do we call a man who pledged to give 99% of his wealth to philanthropy during his lifetime or at death? He is generous and very charitable. He has been supporting the needy and vulnerable in society. So generous is Mr. Buffett that he made history in 2006 by donating $37 billion to the Bill and Melinda Gates Foundation – the largest-ever individual charity donation.

8. He is Modest

The multi-billionaire still lives in the house he bought in the 1950s and is driving a modest car. He does not show off his wealth, neither does he live the lifestyle his fellow billionaires do. He lives comfortably and is quoted saying he does not need money, the society does more.

His modesty is enviable and rare. It makes him stand out from the rest in his pool.

9. He is Selfless

Usually, the rich would want to continue amassing more wealth for themselves as is the practice globally. Mr. Warren is selfless to put the needs of others ahead of their own. This habit is evident in his many generous charitable donations.

10. He Has Enough Sleep

According to the Insider, Mr. Warren Buffett sleeps eight hours a night. He values his time to rest and adheres to it so that he can wake up feeling fresh to face the new day. He wakes up at 6:45 am before reading newspapers.

In conclusion, these ten habits of Warren Buffett form his lifestyle.

Chapter 27:

<u>9 Habits of Successful Students</u>

Successful students are made up of a common DNA. This is because they share a backbone – their success. In the words of Aristotle, *we are what we repeatedly do. Excellence, then, is not an act, but a habit.* Success is a habit that this clique of students has perfected meticulously.

Here are 9 habits of successful students:

1. <u>They Identify With Their Status</u>

It begins at the beginning. It is a paradox in itself. The start of the success of successful students (pun intended) is their acceptance that they are students of whatever discipline they are pursuing. When they correctly identify with their discipline, the journey begins.

Next, they identify with the institution/person under whose tutelage they are placed. Appreciating the expertise of their seniors is as important as it is that they are successful. No one crowns himself King; Kingmakers do crown him or her. In this case, the institution provides the opportunity for the student and teacher to meet.

Successful students, at all levels, identify with their centers of learning. Be it primary school, high school, technical-vocational colleges, or universities, successful students are proud of them (at least during the duration of their study).

2. They Have A Good Attitude

How does the attitude of students connect with their success? Again, why are successful students proud of where they learn? If they have a bad attitude towards their centers of learning, they will dislike their teachers – those responsible for imparting knowledge to them. As a result, whatever they learn will not stick.

Successful students are as good as their attitude is towards their teachers, institutions, and discipline of study. If you want to master your studies then change your attitude. A good attitude opens you up to greater possibilities. The possibilities that will be open to you are infinite.

3. They Relate Well With Their Tutors

The relationship between learners and their teachers should strictly be professional (there is the risk of unethical behavior if it crosses that line). When learners are in harmony with their tutors, learning is easier.

A good relationship between students and teachers breeds trust. Trust is the foundation upon which success is founded. The goodwill of both the teacher and the student is based on the relationship between them. The former being devoted to the latter's needs and the latter submissive to the former's instructions.

Ask top candidates of national examinations how their relationship with their teachers was and you will hear of nothing short of "the best."

4. They Are Willing To Go The Extra Mile

The story of successful students is akin to a fairytale in a fairyland. The prince does everything to protect his bride. He will go the extra mile to make her happy, to know her better, and even to cheer her up. With this infinite love, either of them is ready to move mountains for the sake of the other.

Successful students and their studies are like the groom and bride in the fairyland. The students do not mind going an extra mile for their bride (studies). They study late into the night, sacrifice their free time to grasp new concepts, and are even ready to forego short-time pleasures for the sake of their education.

This sacrifice is what distinguishes them from the rest of their peers.

5. They Are Inquisitive

Successful students are always curious about what they do not know. The unknown stirs curiosity in them; they are never content with the status quo. Their inquisitive nature is gold – a rare characteristic in most students. A majority of them are satisfied with what they know.

Their inquisitiveness births innovation. While settling for nothing short of the best, they try out new practices, re-design existing models and create new inventions. They stand out from their peers. Being inquisitive is not disrespect for authority or existing knowledge. On the contrary, it is appreciating the current principles and building on them to come up with something better.

6. They Have Focus

Their primary goal is clear and everything else is secondary. Successful students have a razor-sharp focus of the eagle, not distracted by anything that crosses their line.

A perfect real-life example is that of a hunting lion. When it settles on its prey from a herd, it chases it to the end. It can even pass other animals while chasing the specific target. The lion does not care whether the animal that crosses its path is better than its target. The only thing that matters is getting to its target.

When students decide to prioritize their education above any other interest, their energy and concentration are drawn to it. Success will be their cup of tea.

7. They Do Their Due Dilligence

The art of assuming is foreign to successful students. They treat everything in their discipline with utmost care. They research on results of experiments and answer the whys that arise.

It is never said by their tutors that they neglected their duty of research. Successful students know their role and they play it well. They know where and when to stop. This makes them disciplined compared to their colleagues.

Their discipline is outstanding. Shape your discipline and you will join the exclusive club of successful students.

8. Abide By The Book

Successful students stick to the rules of the game. This is important since it is not all students who manage to complete the race. Like any other commitment, learning requires agility. It has its own rules, the common and the silent rules. Most important are the unspoken rules that students are expected to abide by.

What is left unsaid, for example, is that students are not expected to be in romantic relationships because it will get in the way of their education.

9. They Are Punctual

Successful students keep time. Punctuality is the backbone of planning which is very important for focused people. Keeping time helps students avoid missing classes and group discussions or arriving very late for the same.

Success itself arrives punctually in the sense that it gives proportionate results to the input invested by those who court it. Successful students are the best timekeepers. Those who do not observe time have learned the hard way how to.

These 9 habits are what successful students do to make it to the top and stay there.

Chapter 28:

8 Ways To Deal With Setbacks In Life

Life is never the same for anyone - It is an ever-changing phenomenon, making you go through all sorts of highs and lows. And as good times are an intrinsic part of your life, so are bad times. One day you might find yourself indebted by 3-digit figures while having only $40 in your savings account. Next day, you might be vacationing in Hawaii because you got a job that you like and pays $100,000 a year. There's absolutely no certainty to life (except passing away) and that's the beauty of it. You never know what is in store for you. But you have to keep living to see it for yourself. Setbacks in life cannot be avoided by anyone. Life will give you hardships, troubles, break ups, diabetes, unpaid bills, stuck toilet and so much more. It's all a part of your life.

Here's 8 ways that you might want to take notes of, for whenever you may find yourself in a difficult position in dealing with setback in life.

1. Accept and if possible, embrace it

The difference between accepting and embracing is that when you accept something, you only believe it to be, whether you agree or disagree. But when you embrace something, you truly KNOW it to be true and accept it as a whole. There is no dilemma or disagreement after you have embraced something.

So, when you find yourself in a difficult situation in life, accept it for what it is and make yourself whole-heartedly believe that this problem in your life, at this specific time, is a part of your life. This problem is what makes you complete. This problem is meant for you and only you can go through it. And you will. Period. There can be no other way.

The sooner you embrace your problem, the sooner you can fix it. Trying to bypass it will only add upon your headaches.

2. Learn from it

Seriously, I can't emphasize how important it is to LEARN from the setbacks you face in your life. Every hardship is a learning opportunity. The more you face challenges, the more you grow. Your capabilities expand with every issue you solve—every difficulty you go through, you rediscover yourself. And when you finally deal off with it, you are reborn. You are a new person with more wisdom and experience.

When you fail at something, try to explore why you failed. Be open-minded about scrutinizing yourself. Why couldn't you overcome a certain situation? Why do you think of this scenario as a 'setback'? The moment you find the answers to these questions is the moment you will have found the solution.

3. Execute What You Have Learnt

The only next step from here is to execute that solution and make sure that the next time you face a similar situation, you'll deal with it by having both your arms tied back and blindfolded. All you have to do is remember what you did in a similar past experience and reapply your previous solution.

Thomas A. Edison, the inventor of the light bulb, failed 10,000 times before finally making it. And he said "I have not failed. I just found 10,000 ways that won't work".

The lesson here is that you have to take every setback as a lesson, that's it.

4. Without shadow, you can never appreciate light

This metaphor is applicable to all things opposite in this universe. Everything has a reciprocal; without one, the other cannot exist. Just as without shadow, we wouldn't have known what light is, similarly, without light, we could've never known about shadow. The two opposites identify and complete each other.

Too much of philosophy class, but to sum it up, your problems in life, ironically, is exactly why you can enjoy your life. For example, if you are a chess player, then defeating other chess players will give you enjoyment while getting defeated will give you distress. But, when you are a chess prodigy—you have defeated every single chess player on earth and there's no one else to defeat, then what will you do to derive pleasure? Truth is, you can now no longer enjoy chess. You have no one to defeat. No one gives you the fear of losing anymore and as a result, the taste of winning has lost its appeal to you.

So, whenever you face a problem in life, appreciate it because without it, you can't enjoy the state of not having a problem. Problems give you the pleasure of learning from them and solving them.

5. View Every Obstacle As an opportunity

This one's especially for long term hindrances to your regular life. The COVID-19 pandemic for instance, has set us back for almost two years now. As distressing it is, there is also some positive impact of it. A long-term setback opens up a plethora of new avenues for you to explore. You suddenly get a large amount of time to experiment with things that you have never tried before.

When you have to pause a regular part of your life, you can do other things in the meantime. I believe that every one of us has a specific talent and most people never know what their talent is simply because they have never tried that thing.

6. Don't Be Afraid to experiment

People pursue their whole life for a job that they don't like and most of them never ever get good at it. As a result, their true talent gets buried under their own efforts. Life just carries on with unfound potential. But when some obstacle comes up and frees you from the clutches of doing what you have been doing for a long time, then you should get around and experiment. Who knows? You, a bored high school teacher, might be a natural at tennis. You won't know it unless you are fired from that job and actually play tennis to get over it. So whenever life gives you lemons, quit trying to hold on to it. Move on and try new things instead.

7. Stop Comparing yourself to others

The thing is, we humans are emotional beings. We become emotionally vulnerable when we are going through something that isn't supposed to be. And in such times, when we see other people doing fantastic things in life, it naturally makes us succumb to more self-loathing. We think lowly of our own selves and it is perfectly normal to feel this way. Talking and comapring ourselves to people who are seemingly untouched by setbacks is a counterproductive move. You will listen to their success-stories and get depressed—lose self-esteem. Even if they try their best to advise you, it won't get through to you. You won't be able to relate to them.

8. Talk to people other people who are having their own setbacks in life

I'm not asking you to talk to just any people. I'm being very specific here: talk to people who are going through bad times as well.

If you start talking to others who are struggling in life, perhaps more so compared to you, then you'll see that everyone else is also having difficulties in life. It will seem natural to you. Moreover, having talked with others might even show you that you are actually doing better than all these other people. You can always find someone who is dealing with more trouble than you and that will enlighten you. That will encourage you. If someone else can deal with tougher setbacks in life, why can't you?

Besides, listening to other people will give you a completely new perspective that you can use for yourself if you ever find yourself in a similar situation as others whom you have talked with.

Conclusion

Setbacks are a part of life. Without them we wouldn't know what the good times are. Without them we wouldn't appreciate the success that we have gotten. Without them we wouldn't cherish the moments that got us to where we are heading to. And without them there wouldn't be any challenge to fill our souls with passion and fire. Take setbacks as a natural process in the journey. Use it to fuel your drive. Use it to move your life forward one step at a time.

Chapter 29:

<u>6 Habits To Impress Your Boss and Thrive</u>

It is still unclear to a majority of people what their bosses and employers want from them. Some expressly make it crystal to their employees their expectations of them while others are reserved. What is clear though, is that bosses worldwide have a common goal – to make a profit. It is the major reason why they hired people in their companies to work for them. Many employees wrongly believe that unless their superiors make a complaint against them, then their work is satisfactory. This notion is a fallacy. Satisfactorily is not the threshold of competency but uniqueness and creativity.

Here are six common habits to impress your boss and thrive:

1. <u>Be Unique And Creative</u>

The question employees fail to answer honestly is what they bring to the table. What is it that makes you stand out in the company you work for? It is not your education level because there are many qualified learned people with your skills. Neither is it the duration you work in the company because you receive remuneration for it.

You should be creative in your work and add value to the company. Your devotion to your work will impress your boss because it is uncommon.

Ideally, you ought to be irreplaceable in your workplace for you to gain favor and earn a promotion.

2. Ensure Proper Communication

Communication is the master key to unlocking conflicts and misunderstandings at the workplace. It is important to ensure proper communication with your boss in your working relationship. You will be able to explain yourself and raise any pertinent issue that affects your work if you have good communication with them.

When you communicate effectively, your superiors will understand you better than if you have poor communication skills or none at all. It may come out as rudeness or ignorance when you communicate ineffectively with your boss. To thrive and gain favor with him/her, build on your communication.

3. Never Outshine Your Master

In his famous book, *48 laws of power*, Robert Greene writes this as his first law. It is prudent never to outshine your master and instead let him appear smarter than you are even if it may not be the case. This speaks life to the respect of hierarchy between your boss and yourself. Never make him appear dumb or lame duck by attracting glory to yourself.

Honor your boss both in your speech and in your actions. This will make you find favor in their eyes and you will thrive in your workplace. It does not imply that you should not give any smart suggestions to your bosses but you should do it in a manner that does not usurp their authority.

4. Have Integrity

Integrity is the quality of honesty and transparency that one may have. You are misplaced and out of order if your boss cannot trust you to do a task without supervision. Worse is that you are in a bad light if you fall short of honesty and cannot be trusted with the management of resources.

Leaders and bosses are universally interested in people of integrity who will fairly work for them. They want people they will trust to oversee the rest and take their organizations to the next level. The lack of integrity is the biggest turn-off for bosses no matter how qualified employees could be. Uphold integrity to impress your boss and you shall thrive.

5. Share Their Vision For The Company

The hiring of managers is tedious and sometimes the competent candidates could not be having the passion of the business at heart. Their remunerations could be their greatest motivation. Routine checks and job evaluations could reveal such hidden traits in employees.

Nevertheless, you need to share the vision of the company with your employer for them to trust you with their resources. People who share the company vision impress hiring managers and owners because their salary is not the sole motivation to work.

6. Be Punctual

It is prudent to be punctual in your job. Punctuality is the act of being on time, never late for anything. You should report to work on time, complete assigned tasks on time, and even submit reports required from you on time.

Being punctual is a sign of dedication to your job. This act alone will make your boss have a soft spot for you.

In conclusion, when you develop these six habits, you will impress your boss and thrive at your workplace.

Chapter 30:

5 Ways To Adopt Right Attitude For Success

Being successful is a few elements that require hard work, dedication, and a positive attitude. It requires building your resilience and having a clear idea of your future ahead. Though it might be hard to decide your life forward, a reasonable manner is something that comes naturally to those who are willing to give their all. Adopting a new attitude doesn't always mean to change yourself in a way but, it has more meaning towards changing your mindset to an instinct. That is when you get stressed or overworked is because of an opposing point of view on life.

With success comes a great sense of dealing with things. You become more professional, and you feel the need to achieve more in every aspect. Don't be afraid to be power-hungry. But, it also doesn't mean to be unfair. Try to go for a little more than before, each step ahead. Make your hard work or talent count in every aspect. Make yourself a successful person in a positive manner, so you'll find yourself making the most of yourself. And don't give up on the things you need in life.

1. **Generate Pragmatic Impressions**

"The first impression is the last impression." It's true that once you've introduced yourself to the person in front of you, there is only a tiny chance that you'll get to introduce yourself again. So, choosing the correct wording while creating an impression is a must. You need to be optimistic about yourself and inform the other person about you in a way that influences them. An impression that leaves an effect on them, so they will willingly meet you again. A person must be kind and helpful towards its inferior and respectful towards their superior. This is one of the main characteristics for a person to be a successful man or woman. And with a negative attitude, the opposite occurs. People are more inclined to work without you. They nearly never consider you to work with them and try to contact you as little as possible. So, a good impression is significant.

2. Be True To Your Words

Choose your wording very carefully, because once said, it can't be taken back. Also, for a successful life, commitment is always an important rule. Be true to what you said to a person. Make them believe that they can trust you comfortably. So, it would be best if you chose your words. Don't commit if you can't perform. False commitment leads to loss of customers and leads to the loss of your impression as a successful worker. Always make sure that you fulfill your commands and promises to your clients and make them satisfied with your performance. It leads to a positive mindset and a dedication to work towards your goal.

3. A Positive Personal Life

Whatever you may be doing in your professional life can impact your personal life too. Creating the right mindset professionally also helps you to keep a positive attitude at home. It allows you to go forward with the proper consultation with your heart. It will make you happier. You'll desire to achieve more in life because you'll be satisfied with your success. It will push to go furthermore. It will drive you towards the passion for desiring more. Hard work and determination will continue to be your support, and you will be content will your heart. By keeping a good attitude, you'll be helping yourself more than helping others.

4. Be Aggressive and Determined

Becoming goal-oriented is one of the main factors evolving success in your life. If you are not determined to do your work, you'll just accept things the way others present you. It will leave you in misery and deeply dissatisfied with yourself. Similarly, you'll tend to do something more your way if you are goal-oriented and not how others want. You'll want to shale everything according to your need, and you become delighted with yourself and the result of your hard work. Always keep a clear view of your next step as it will form you in to your true self. Don't just go with the flow, but try to change it according to your wants and needs.

5. Create Your Master Plan

Indeed, we can't achieve great things with only hard work. We will always need to add a factor or to in our business. But by imagining or strategizing, some plans might be helpful. With hard work and some solid projects, we will get our desired outcome. If not, at least we get something close. And if you chose the wrong option, then the amount of hard work won't matter. You'll never get what you want no matter the hard work. So, always make sure to make plans strategically.

Conclusion

By keeping a positive attitude, you'll not only be helpful to others but to yourself too. Make sure you keep the proper manner—a manner required to be a successful person. Do lots of achievements and try to prove yourself as much as possible. Try keeping a good impact on people around you in everything you do. Have the spirit and courage to achieve great heights. And be sure to make moat of yourself. Consistency is the key.

CPSIA information can be obtained
at www.ICGtesting.com
Printed in the USA
LVHW051549140122
708430LV00013B/609

9 789814 952644